はじめに

2012年4月に出版された *Achieve Your Best on the TOEIC® Test* はお蔭様で好評をいただきました。大学における一回の授業内でリスニング、リーディングを基礎からテーマ別にバランスよく学習できることを特徴としているテキストです。本書はその改訂版として作成され　　　　　　　基本構成は変えていません。半年から一年の学習で600点をクリアす　　　　　　　　　　　　題傾向に沿った内容を効率的に学ぶことができるよう配慮していま　　　　　　　　　　　留意したことは、以下のとおりです。

》》 TOEIC® L&R頻出ボキャブラリー

TOEIC® L&Rは英語での実務経験のない大学生にとっては知らない語彙がたくさん出てきます。従って各ユニットの冒頭では各テーマに必要な基本語彙についてディクテーションをしながら学ぶ形式になっています。

Part 1 人の動作のみならず、物の状態、風景の描写、現在進行受動態 (being＋過去分詞) 、現在完了形など写真描写問題に出題される全てのパターンを網羅しました。

Part 2 疑問詞の質問や、依頼の表現、平叙文などの頻出問題を出題しています。返答を保留にする回答が正解になる問題も多く取り入れており、本番に近い出題を意識しました。

Part 3 及び **Part 4** TOEIC® L&Rで出題頻度の高いトピックスを中心に構成しています。セリフの意図を問う問題やグラフィック (図版問題) 問題も出題しています。

Part 5 文法問題は、品詞・動詞・助動詞・接続詞などの基本頻出パターンに絞っています。また、テーマに沿った語彙を問題に取り入れることで語彙習得の効果を高めています。

Part 6 頻出のテーマのみに絞って出題しています。文法のルールで判断して解く文法問題だけでなく、前後の文脈 (context) を考えて解く語彙問題や文章挿入問題も出題しています。

Part 7 TOEIC® L&Rテストと同様、文章全体の趣旨と流れを把握した上で解答する問題を意識的に増やしました。

本書は、TOEIC® L&Rの総合学習教材として全パートをカバーするように編集されています。大学等でのクラスでの使用はもちろん、授業後の自己学習書としても充分活用できる内容となっています。
本書を通して多くの学習者が英語力を向上させることを期待しています。

2024年3月

著者一同

TOEIC® L&R とは何か

TOEIC®（Test of English for International Communication）は、米国のテスト開発機関ETS（Educational Testing Service）が開発した国際コミュニケーション英語能力テストです。問題はリスニングセクション（約45分間100問）と、リーディングセクション（75分間100問）からなり、全体2時間で200問のマークシート方式の一斉客観テストです。配点は、リスニング、リーディングそれぞれ5点〜495点、合計10点〜990点の点数幅があり、5点刻みで点数が表示されます。問題の構成は以下のように設定されています。

リスニングセクション（約45分間）		
パート 1（写真描写問題）	1-6	6問
パート 2（応答問題）	7-31	25問
パート 3（会話問題）	32-70	39問
パート 4（説明文問題）	71-100	30問
合　計		100問

リーディングセクション（75分間）		
パート 5（短文空埋め問題）	101-130	30問
パート 6（長文空埋め問題）	131-146	16問
パート 7（読解問題）	147-200	54問
合　計		100問

参考資料：一般財団法人 国際ビジネスコミュニケーション協会

https://www.iibc-global.org/toeic.html ▶

本書の特徴

本書は、TOEIC® L&R総合学習教材であり、TOEIC® L&Rの全パートをカバーしています。本書の特徴は以下のとおりです。

≫ テーマ別のユニット構成

TOEIC® L&R頻出テーマである旅行、オフィス、レストラン、メディア、健康、不動産・住宅、ショッピング、就職活動、天気・環境、娯楽・スポーツ、会議に関するシーンをユニットごとにまとめています。

≫ 頻出ボキャブラリー

各テーマのTOEIC® L&R頻出ボキャブラリーをユニットの冒頭で学べる構成になっています。最初は音声を聴いてディクテーションしてください。その後、文を読み内容を理解した上で、語彙を覚えるまで音源と共に繰り返しオーバーラッピングやリピート練習をしましょう。シャドーイング練習も効果的です。脳内で母語に訳すプロセスを経ることなく英語のまま聞き取ることができるようになり、リスニングセクションの各パートにおける対応スピードがアップするはずです。

≫ コモントピックスを選定

TOEIC® L&Rの各パートの中で、何度も繰り返し出題されるトピックスが存在します。それらのうち代表的なテーマを厳選して問題を作成しましたので、テストに備えて話の流れ、頻出単語・表現を覚えておくと非常に効果的です。

≫ 多様な英語の発音に対応

TOEIC® L&Rのリスニングセクションでは、アメリカ英語のみならず、イギリス、カナダ、オーストラリアで話されている英語を発音するスピーカーによって構成されています。従って本書でもTOEIC® L&Rの本番に沿った多様なスピーカーで音声録音をおこないました。

本書を通して、多くの学習者がTOEIC® L&Rで目標にしている高得点を取得し、英語学習のステップアップに繋げていただければ幸いです。

目次

Contents

旅行①

TOEIC® L&Rでは、リスニングでもリーディングでも旅行に関する問題が必ず出題されます。空港、駅、バスターミナル、機内アナウンス、ホテル、旅行代理店とのメールのやりとりなど、旅行に関する表現に慣れておくとよいでしょう。

≫ TOEIC® L&R頻出ボキャブラリーチェック

▶ホテルで 🔊 Audio ① 02

1. We encourage you to _____ your room _____ _____ during the holiday season.
   ホリデーシーズンは事前にご予約されることをお勧めいたします。

2. _____ services are available to make your travel more relaxing.
   ご旅行をより快適にするための無料サービスをご用意しております。

▶空港で

3. Flights have _____ _____ due to the adverse weather conditions.
   悪天候のためフライトに遅れが出ています。

4. The flight time _____ London _____ Tokyo is _____ 12 hours.
   ロンドンから東京までの飛行時間は約12時間です。

5. Most airlines allow one piece of luggage that can fit in the _____ _____.
   ほとんどの航空会社では、頭上の荷物入れに入る手荷物は1個までです。

6. All passengers are kindly asked to _____ their seatbelts and switch off their devices for the _____ of the flight.
   乗客の皆様にはシートベルトを着用いただき、飛行中は機器の電源を切ってください。

▶旅行中によく使われる表現

7. The _____ _____ is only _____ to tickets purchased at the hotel reception.
   割引料金は、ホテルのフロントで購入したチケットにのみ適用されます。

8. Members should carry their membership cards and official _____ documents.
   会員の方は会員証と公的な身分証明書を携帯してください。

9. You can search for a route to your _____ with this app.
   このアプリを使えば目的地までのルートを検索することができます。

10. This is our recommended _____ for nature-lovers in summer.
    こちらは夏の自然を愛する人たちにお勧めの旅程です。

11. The _____ ticket gives you full access to all attractions in the park.
    入場券には、園内のすべてのアトラクションの利用が含まれています。

>> Photographs 🔊 Audio ① 03-04

Part 1 Please listen to four statements about a photograph. When you hear the statements, you must select one statement from (A), (B), (C), or (D) that best describes the photograph.

1. (A) (B) (C) (D)

2. (A) (B) (C) (D)

>> Question-Response 🔊 Audio ① 05-06

Part 2 Please listen to a question or statement and three responses spoken in English. Then, choose the best response to the question or statement from (A), (B), or (C).

3. (A) (B) (C)
4. (A) (B) (C)
5. (A) (B) (C)
6. (A) (B) (C)

≫ Short Conversations 🔊 Audio ① 07-09

Part 3 Please listen to a short conversation between two or more people. You must listen carefully to understand what the speakers say. You are to choose the best answer to each question.

7. What will happen tomorrow?
   (A) The woman is going to Orlando, Florida.
   (B) The woman will get married.
   (C) People will celebrate Thanksgiving.
   (D) The woman will deal with something important.

8. What is the relationship between the two speakers?
   (A) Best friends   (C) Lunchmates
   (B) Office colleagues   (D) Husband and wife

9. What does the man suggest to her?
   (A) Leave her workplace right now   (C) Get out of the office when she can
   (B) Take the subway to avoid traffic (D) Fly directly to Orlando

≫ Short Talks 🔊 Audio ① 10-12

Part 4 Please listen to a short talk. You must listen carefully to understand and remember what is said. You are to choose the best answer to each question.

10. Where is the final destination of this flight?
    (A) Hong Kong   (C) Pacific Islands
    (B) San Francisco   (D) Japan

11. After how many minutes will the flight leave?
    (A) Four minutes   (C) Ten minutes
    (B) Seven minutes   (D) Three minutes

12. What is the last thing passengers are asked to do for take-off?
    (A) Fasten their seatbelts
    (B) Keep all baggage underneath their seats
    (C) Turn off all personal electronic devices
    (D) Not to smoke during the flight

>> Text Completion

Part 6 Select the best choice to complete the text.

Questions 13-16 refer to the following notice.

Important notes:

All visitors must show their tickets, including those entitled to free ------- .
13.
If you choose a free or ------- price ticket, you will need to prove your
14.
right to the discount by presenting the appropriate documentation. If
you are registered with ------- program, you do not need to buy tickets
15.
of any kind. You can go straight to the park's entrances and show your
identification to enter. ------- .
16.

---

13. (A) toll
　(B) fine
　(C) admission
　(D) fare

14. (A) reduced
　(B) reduces
　(C) reducing
　(D) to reduce

15. (A) ourselves
　(B) our
　(C) we
　(D) us

16. (A) If you have a reservation for 9:30,
　　you can enter the park until 10:00.
　(B) Our travel schedule includes a
　　visit to the New Central Park.
　(C) In case of adverse weather
　　conditions, the optional tour will
　　be canceled.
　(D) Should you have any questions,
　　please feel free to contact our
　　Visitor Attention Service.

>> Reading Comprehension

Questions 17-18 refer to the following notice.

Membership No. 3013409xxxxxx Gold

Discover Your Own Crane Hill

Hello, Mr. Yamamoto,

Welcome back to Hong Kong!

It's time to plan your next trip and reconnect with everything you love about this dynamic city, from authentic street food to internationally acclaimed restaurants, cultural areas, retail centers, vibrant nightlife and the stunning Victoria Harbour.

Everything you've missed is within reach when you stay with us.

Explore Your Room Reservation

---

17. What is the purpose of the notice?
(A) To request an extended stay
(B) To express the deepest apologies
(C) To make a list of travel destinations
(D) To encourage a room booking

18. What is indicated about Mr. Yamamoto?
(A) He is working for a travel agency.
(B) He has not visited Hong Kong before.
(C) He is a valuable member of the hotel.
(D) He owns an authentic restaurant there.

Unit

1

旅
行
①

▶Incomplete Sentences as REVIEW TEST

Part 5 Select the best choice to complete the sentence.

19. Here is a suggestion for an ------- allowing you to explore Italy in just two weeks.
    (A) itinerary
    (B) arrival
    (C) orientation
    (D) extension

20. Due to a mechanical problem, all trains to Dublin -------.
    (A) have delayed
    (B) were delaying
    (C) to delay
    (D) were delayed

21. You are allowed to bring two ------- of baggage with you on this airline carrier.
    (A) pieces
    (B) packages
    (C) pairs
    (D) sheets

22. These ------- cards are available to residents who do not have a driver's license.
    (A) identifying
    (B) identification
    (C) identified
    (D) identifiable

23. Please ------- your seatbelts when you are seated at all times during the flight.
    (A) make
    (B) fasten
    (C) pull
    (D) take

24. During the fall tourist season, it is recommended to reserve flights ------- advance.
    (A) at
    (B) on
    (C) in
    (D) by

25. The travel agency offers a wide range of ------- recognized destinations for tourists.
    (A) internationalize
    (B) internationalization
    (C) international
    (D) internationally

オフィス ①

TOEIC® L&Rで設問に使われるトピックスは、ビジネスにおける状況（business settings）に関連していることが多いです。したがって、オフィスでの従業員同士の会話表現、社内の業務連絡（memorandum）、社外へのレターなどに関する表現に慣れておきましょう。

▶ TOEIC® L&R頻出ボキャブラリーチェック

▶会議で 🔊 Audio ① 13

1. Before we get started, please check the _____ meeting's _____.
   始める前に、前回の議事録を確認してください。

2. Could you _____ more research on _____ in our target market?
   ターゲットとする市場の競合他社について、更に調査してもらえませんか？

3. That company has great _____ for _____ and success.
   その会社は発展と飛躍の大きな可能性を秘めています。

4. Our company has been a leader in the industry _____ _____.
   我が社は、何十年にもわたって業界をリードしてきました。

▶手紙、Eメールで

5. We would _____ it if you could attend the conference.
   その会議にご出席いただければありがたいです。

6. We are pleased to announce plans to _____ a new product in the third _____.
   第3四半期に新製品を発売する予定であることをお知らせします。

▶オフィスでよく使われる表現

7. I'm _____ _____ _____ office supplies.
   私は備品の管理を担当しています。

8. He has the authority to _____ all expense reports.
   彼にはすべての経費報告書を承認する権限があります。

9. The report _____ _____ _____ be submitted by the end of the week.
   週明けには報告書を提出することになっています。

10. She was offered a _____ _____ team leader due to her exceptional leadership skills.
    彼女はその卓越した指導力が評価され、チームリーダーへの昇進を提示されました。

≫ **Photographs** 📶 Audio ① 14-15

Part 1 Please listen to four statements about a photograph. When you hear the statements, you must select one statement from (A), (B), (C), or (D) that best describes the photograph.

1. Ⓐ Ⓑ Ⓒ Ⓓ   2. Ⓐ Ⓑ Ⓒ Ⓓ

≫ **Question-Response** 📶 Audio ① 16-17

Part 2 Please listen to a question or statement and three responses spoken in English. Then, choose the best response to the question or statement from (A), (B), or (C).

3. Ⓐ Ⓑ Ⓒ
4. Ⓐ Ⓑ Ⓒ
5. Ⓐ Ⓑ Ⓒ
6. Ⓐ Ⓑ Ⓒ

≫ Short Conversations 🔊 Audio① 18-20

Part 3 Please listen to a short conversation between two or more people. You must listen carefully to understand what the speakers say. You are to choose the best answer to each question.

7. What do the women think about the man?
   (A) He seems too angry.
   (B) He seems very tired.
   (C) He looks pale due to sickness.
   (D) He appears happy with things.

8. What does Susan suggest the man do tomorrow?
   (A) He should talk to his manager.
   (B) He should take a vacation.
   (C) He should hire another person.
   (D) He should try to keep the costs down.

9. What is the man's problem?
   (A) He might lose his job.
   (B) He has too much work.
   (C) His boss hates him.
   (D) He needs to reduce costs.

≫ Short Talks 🔊 Audio① 21-23

Part 4 Please listen to a short talk. You must listen carefully to understand and remember what is said. You are to choose the best answer to each question.

10. What is the main topic of the talk?
   (A) How to build good team relationships with employees
   (B) How to give an effective speech to employees
   (C) What to say at a wedding celebration
   (D) What speech topics you should or should not use

11. Who might be the speaker?
   (A) A manager
   (B) A new employee
   (C) A conference keynote speaker
   (D) A speech training professional

12. What advice does the speaker have for participants?
   (A) Make the speech dramatic
   (B) Keep the speech simple
   (C) Consider time, place, and occasion
   (D) Do not read directly from speech notes

Reading Parts

>> Reading Comprehension

Part 7 Choose the best answer, (A), (B), (C), or (D), to each question.

Questions 13-15 refer to the following minutes.

Date: June 4
Time: 10:00 A.M.
Location: Conference Room 3
Attendees: John Smith (Chairperson), Sarah Lee, Tom Brown, Emma Davis, David Kim

---

Agenda:
1. Review of the previous meeting's minutes
2. Presentation of the sales report
3. Discussion of the upcoming product launch
4. Any other business issues

Minutes:
1. The chairman reviewed the minutes of the previous meeting, and they were approved.
2. The sales report was presented by David Kim. He reported a double increase in sales compared to the previous quarter. The company's new marketing strategy and promotional activities were attributed to this increase in sales. The team congratulated David on his successful efforts.
3. The upcoming product launch was discussed in detail. Tom Brown shared his ideas regarding the product's packaging design, and Sarah Lee discussed the marketing campaign. Emma Davis talked about the possible target market, and the team discussed the potential competitors. The team concluded that they need to conduct more research on the target audience and competitors.
4. There were no other business issues to discuss.

13. Who took a leadership role in the meeting?
(A) John Smith
(B) Tom Brown
(C) Emma Davis
(D) David Kim

14. What was the sales increase reported in the meeting?
(A) 10%
(C) 100%
(B) 50%
(D) 200%

15. What was discussed in the meeting about the product launch?
(A) A TV commercial
(C) An alternative business partner
(B) The previous sales meeting
(D) The target audience

Questions 16-17 refer to the following letter.

Dear Mr. Brian Carter,
Congratulations on your recent promotion to Creative Director.

I know you have worked hard to earn this recognition for two decades at Sloan Curtis, and I feel that they are very wise in having made this choice.

We had the great opportunity to work with the previous Creative Director, Teddy Mall. Of course, it is sad to see him leave, but we look forward to working even closer with you in the coming years.

We are also happy to learn of your replacement as Assistant Creative Director, Doug Hallanoug. He has some big shoes to fill, but we are sure he will do well.

Please accept our best wishes for your success in your new position.

Sincerely,
Ben Sharon

16. What is the purpose of this letter?
(A) To celebrate a promotion
(B) To recognize his new business
(C) To accept his apology
(D) To apply for a job

17. How many years has Brian Carter worked for the company?
(A) Ten years
(C) Twenty years
(B) Fifteen years
(D) Twenty-five years

Incomplete Sentences as REVIEW TEST

Part 5 Select the best choice to complete the sentence.

18. The secretary was responsible for taking the ------- during the conference call.
(A) agenda
(B) minutes
(C) lecture
(D) proposal

19. Our team ------- a survey to gather feedback from our customers on our new product.
(A) accomplished
(B) underwent
(C) placed
(D) conducted

20. I am afraid that it is ------- to rain this afternoon.
(A) suppose
(B) supposed
(C) supposing
(D) being supposed

21. The IT Department is ------- charge of maintaining the company's network and computer systems.
(A) in
(B) at
(C) by
(D) on

22. I want to express my ------- for your hard work and dedication to this project.
(A) appreciated
(B) appreciate
(C) appreciation
(D) appreciative

23. Congratulations on your recent ------- to vice president.
(A) promoting
(B) promotion
(C) promote
(D) promoted

24. The board of directors has ------- the new budget proposal.
(A) approved
(B) apologized
(C) agreed
(D) appreciated

レストラン

TOEIC® L&Rでは、レストランに関する表現が出題されます。店員との会話、メニュー、レシピ、レセプション、パーティーなどの設定場面はある程度限られているので、表現を事前にインプットしておけばさほど難しくありません。レストランで使われる表現に慣れておくとよいでしょう。

≫ TOEIC® L&R頻出ボキャブラリーチェック

▶客同士の会話　🔊 Audio ① 24

1. After a long day of sightseeing, I think we all have big _____ today.
   一日中観光したので、今日はみんな食欲旺盛だと思います。

2. The _____ on the menu seem quite _____.
   メニューの値段はかなりお手頃のようです。

3. Do you have any vegetarian options _____ on the menu?
   ベジタリアン向けのメニューはありますか？

4. Please let me know _____ _____ _____ the soup of the day contains any gluten.
   本日のスープにグルテンが含まれているかどうか教えてください。

5. This restaurant is known for serving _____ Italian cuisine at _____ prices.
   このレストランは本格的なイタリア料理を手頃な値段で提供することで知られています。

▶店員との会話

6. I _____ you _____ _____ the braised beef short ribs.
   牛ショートリブの煮込みをお勧めします。

7. This dessert is made with carefully selected, high-quality _____.
   こちらのデザートは厳選された上質な素材を使用しております。

8. Our chef has trained _____ in Japanese _____.
   当店のシェフは、日本料理の修行を幅広く積んでいます。

9. We _____ your _____. This is _____ _____ _____.
   ご愛顧いただきありがとうございます。こちらは店のおごりです。

10. We _____ currently _____ _____ staff, so the service might be a bit slower than usual.
    現在、スタッフ不足のため、通常より少し提供が遅くなるかもしれません。

11. I'd _____ _____ _____ recommend some wine pairings for your meal this evening.
    今晩のお食事に合うワインのペアリングを喜んでおすすめいたします。

▶ Listening Parts

≫ Photographs 🔊 Audio ① 25-26

Part 1 Please listen to four statements about a photograph. When you hear the statements, you must select one statement from (A), (B), (C), or (D) that best describes the photograph.

1. Ⓐ Ⓑ Ⓒ Ⓓ

2. Ⓐ Ⓑ Ⓒ Ⓓ

≫ Question-Response 🔊 Audio ① 27-28

Part 2 Please listen to a question or statement and three responses spoken in English. Then, choose the best response to the question or statement from (A), (B), or (C).

3. Ⓐ Ⓑ Ⓒ
4. Ⓐ Ⓑ Ⓒ
5. Ⓐ Ⓑ Ⓒ
6. Ⓐ Ⓑ Ⓒ

>> Short Conversations 🔊 Audio ① 29-31

Part 3   Please listen to a short conversation between two or more people. You must listen carefully to understand what the speakers say. You are to choose the best answer to each question.

7. Where most likely are the speakers?
   (A) At a farmer's market
   (B) At a grocery store
   (C) At a restaurant
   (D) At a supermarket

8. When does this conversation take place?
   (A) Before the dinner course
   (B) During the dinner course
   (C) After the dinner course
   (D) After dessert

9. What will the woman have next?
   (A) Vanilla ice cream
   (B) Chocolate chip cookies
   (C) A cup of coffee
   (D) Lemon sherbet

>> Short Talks 🔊 Audio ① 32-34

Part 4   Please listen to a short talk. You must listen carefully to understand and remember what is said. You are to choose the best answer to each question.

10. Who might be the speaker?
    (A) Chef Rudy
    (B) The shop owner
    (C) A reporter
    (D) A travel guide presenter

11. What makes Chicago-style pizza different?
    (A) The special tomato sauce
    (B) The thick crust
    (C) The sliced cheese
    (D) The reasonable price

12. What will the listener do next?
    (A) Enter the shop
    (B) Learn its history
    (C) Eat the pizza
    (D) Order pizza online

≫ Text Completion

Part 6 Select the best choice to complete the text.

Questions 13-16 refer to the following e-mail.

Dear Tiger Diner,

I am writing to request a reservation for the dinner and floor show that ------
13.
by your restaurant on May 20th. It is for a group of eight.

We have heard wonderful things about your restaurant's ------ floor show,
14.
and we would be delighted to experience it while enjoying a delicious meal.

------. Could you please confirm if you have availability for the requested
15.
date and seats?

We would appreciate it if you could confirm the availability of the reservation
as soon as possible.

Thank you for your attention to this matter ------.
16.

Best regards,
Robert Stark

---

13. (A) will offer   (B) had been offered   (C) is offering   (D) is offered

14. (A) enthusiastic   (B) excited   (C) renowned   (D) appetizing

15. (A) I would like our party to be seated towards the middle of your restaurant.
   (B) I would also like to know whether the restaurant offers a shuttle service
      or not.
   (C) I would like to cancel due to a member of our party not being able to make it.
   (D) You should decide exactly when you would like to eat there.

16. (A) before   (C) in person
   (B) in advance   (D) at least

≫ Reading Comprehension

Part 7 Choose the best answer, (A), (B), (C), or (D), to each question.

Questions 17-20 refer to the following notice.

OVER 200 ITEMS WHICH INCLUDE:
Snow Crab Legs, Mussels, Clams, Shrimp Cocktail, Sushi, Pizza, Duck, Grilled Fish, and many other
Chinese, American, Italian, and Japanese Selections, Desserts, Salad, Soup ... and much more!

Are you looking for cuisine that's both authentic and affordable? Are you having trouble deciding where to take the family, with a comfortable, friendly atmosphere in mind, but have no idea what will satisfy their appetites? Then we encourage you to come down to **China Buffet**, where we have over 200 dishes of Chinese, American, Italian, and Japanese cuisine that will have your mouth watering before you even step in our doors. From an open BBQ grill to sushi, we have an assortment of tasty selections, prepared by chefs with the experience and background to demand perfection from themselves and those around them. We also have some delicious vegetarian dishes available, for those with specific diets. We even offer spacious party rooms for those special occasions where our eclectic selection of food is just what you need for your birthdays, reunions, or meetings. If you're still not convinced, then come down to our restaurant today, and witness for yourself our ability to please!

Open Hours
〈Lunch〉 Monday to Saturday   10:30 A.M. to 3:00 P.M.
〈Dinner〉 Monday to Thursday   3:00 P.M. to 10:00 P.M.
　　　　　 Friday & Saturday   3:00 P.M. to 11:00 P.M.
Sunday ALL DAY   11:00 A.M. to 10:00 P.M.

China Buffet
5393 E. 82nd Street, Indianapolis, IN 46250 USA
Phone# (317) 578-7888 Fax# (317) 578-2888

Unit 3 レストラン

17. What is the earliest time to have lunch on Sunday?
   (A) 10:00 A.M.
   (B) 10:30 A.M.
   (C) 11:00 A.M.
   (D) 10:00 P.M.

18. What kind of restaurant is China Buffet?
   (A) Authentic Chinese restaurant
   (B) Oriental restaurant
   (C) Casual international restaurant
   (D) Asian restaurant

19. Who might be the restaurant's main customers?
   (A) Honeymoon couples
   (B) Families
   (C) Foreign visitors
   (D) Elderly people

20. What service does this restaurant also provide?
   (A) Breakfast buffet
   (B) Dancing
   (C) Live music
   (D) Party facilities

▶ Incomplete Sentences as REVIEW TEST

Part 5 Select the best choice to complete the sentence.

21. The chef's special is a hearty beef stew that is sure to satisfy your -------.
   (A) cuisine   (C) meal
   (B) appetite   (D) option

22. We encourage our customers ------- our chef's specials for a delicious dining experience.
   (A) trying   (C) tried
   (B) to try   (D) are trying

23. The authentic Italian pizza at this restaurant is made with the freshest -------.
(A) ingredients
(B) flavors
(C) parts
(D) materials

24. We would ------- it if you could accommodate our request for a table by the window.
(A) be appreciative
(B) appreciating
(C) appreciate
(D) be appreciated

25. Could you tell me ------- the fish dish is spicy or not?
(A) which
(B) either
(C) whether
(D) neither

26. We can enjoy local dishes that are authentic to the region but still ------- in price.
(A) costly
(B) effective
(C) economical
(D) affordable

27. We are currently ------- on avocado, so we cannot add it as an ingredient to your salad.
(A) short
(B) lack
(C) insufficient
(D) out

メディア

TOEIC® L&Rでは、新聞・雑誌・広告に関する問題が出題されます。特にリスニングパートでは、豪雨や洪水といった災害、交通渋滞などのレポート、リーディングパートでは、雑誌の定期購読の申し込み、書評、ソーシャルメディアなどの出題パターンがあります。

 TOEIC® L&R頻出ボキャブラリーチェック

▶雑誌・新聞・オンラインメディアの講読　🔊 Audio ① 35

1. This _____ _____ offers on-demand learning content.
   このストリーミング・サービスは、オンデマンドで学習コンテンツを配信しています。

2. _____ _____ Global News by _____ _____ for our service.
   当社サービスにご登録いただくと、Global Newsが購読できます。

3. To _____ a wider audience, we aim to expand its content library.
   より多くの方にご覧いただくため、内容の充実を目指します。

▶オンライン広告

4. We plan to _____ our service _____ various social media platforms.
   様々なSNSを通じて本サービスを販売促進する予定です。

5. The marketing team _____ _____ _____ on relevant websites.
   マーケティングチームは関連サイトに広告を出しました。

6. Influencers endorsing our service on social media _____ _____ _____.
   当社のサービスをSNSで支持するインフルエンサーのおかげで話題性が出ました。

▶編集について

7. You must _____ the _____ by the _____ _____.
   締め切りまでに記事を投稿しなければなりません。

8. The _____ _____ of the article needs further _____.
   記事の原稿の下書きは、さらに編集が必要です。

9. The author _____ the final draft to _____ _____.
   著者は編集長に最終原稿を提出しました。

10. The publisher announced plans to _____ the errors in the latest edition.
    出版社は最新版の誤植を修正する予定であると発表しました。

▶ Listening Parts

≫ Photographs 🔊 Audio ① 36-37

Part 1 Please listen to four statements about a photograph. When you hear the statements, you must select one statement from (A), (B), (C), or (D) that best describes the photograph.

1. Ⓐ Ⓑ Ⓒ Ⓓ

2. Ⓐ Ⓑ Ⓒ Ⓓ

≫ Question-Response 🔊 Audio ① 38-39

Part 2 Please listen to a question or statement and three responses spoken in English. Then, choose the best response to the question or statement from (A), (B), or (C).

3. Ⓐ Ⓑ Ⓒ
4. Ⓐ Ⓑ Ⓒ
5. Ⓐ Ⓑ Ⓒ
6. Ⓐ Ⓑ Ⓒ

>> Short Conversations 🔊 Audio ① 40-42

Part 3 Please listen to a short conversation between two or more people. You must listen carefully to understand what the speakers say. You are to choose the best answer to each question.

7. What is the topic of the conversation?
   (A) A new company policy
   (B) Horror stories
   (C) Social media posts
   (D) Employee firings

8. Why is the company sending out the new information?
   (A) To control what employees say
   (B) To protect the company's copyright
   (C) To promote social media use
   (D) To increase employee engagement

9. Why does the woman say, "Makes sense."?
   (A) To explain the media policy
   (B) To agree with the man
   (C) To confidently promote the new policy
   (D) To make sure confidential matter

>> Short Talks 🔊 Audio ① 43-45

Part 4 Please listen to a short talk. You must listen carefully to understand and remember what is said. You are to choose the best answer to each question.

10. Who might be the speaker?
   (A) A digital marketing specialist
   (B) A professional accountant
   (C) A job applicant
   (D) A personnel director

11. What is the topic of the talk?
   (A) The rise of social media
   (B) The benefits of online advertising
   (C) The impact of Internet advertisement
   (D) The importance of ad-blockers

12. What are some advantages of online advertising?
   (A) The ability to focus on desired customer base
   (B) The popularity of video ads in streaming content
   (C) The use of ad-blockers for customer protection
   (D) The ability to merge with social media

>> Reading Comprehension

Part 7 Choose the best answer, (A), (B), (C), or (D), to each question.

Questions 13-17 refer to the following article and e-mail.

Netmovies, the world's leading streaming service, has announced plans to launch a new series based on the bestselling novel *The Girl on the Bus* by Stacy Jones. The thriller will be made into an eight-episode series and is set to appear later this year.

The novel, which was released 5 years ago, tells the story of Jennifer Smith, a bus passenger who becomes involved in a murder investigation after seeing a shocking incident from the bus window. The book was a success, selling over 24 million copies worldwide and translated into 38 languages.

The series will star Ashley Bluntberry and is being produced by Dream Forever Television. The announcement has generated significant buzz among fans of the book and Netmovies subscribers alike, with many eagerly anticipating the series' release.

In a statement, Netmovies' Vice President of Original Series expressed excitement for the upcoming project, saying that *The Girl on the Bus* is an exciting story that has captivated readers around the world, and we're happy to bring it to the screen. The announcement is part of Netmovies' recent efforts to expand its original content and attract new subscribers. The streaming company has enjoyed success recently with hit shows such as *Stranger Times* and *The Queen's Crown,* and the company said that it intends to continue making high-quality original programming.

To: hollywoodtoday@inquiries.co.us
From: keikoforester@netmovies.com
Date: Thursday, April 16
Subject: Netmovies Article on April 13 Homepage

To whom it may concern,

I am writing to you regarding your recent Netmovies article. — [1] —. While we appreciate the interest in our upcoming series shown on the Hollywood Today website, we would like to address a couple of errors in the article.

Firstly, the title of the novel is *Girl on a Bus*, not *The Girl on the Bus*. — [2] —. This is surprising considering how popular the book is. We kindly request that you make the correction in the article.

Secondly, the article says that the series will be produced by Dream Forever, which is not accurate. The series is being produced in-house by Netmovies. — [3] —.

Finally, a small point: it's 38 million copies sold and in 24 languages.

— [4] —. We believe that accuracy in reporting is crucial, and we hope that you can make the necessary corrections to the article.

Thank you for your attention to this matter.

Best regards,

Keiko Forester
Media Relations Manager
Netmovies Inc.

13. What is the article mainly about?
    (A) A new best-selling fiction book
    (B) A new media company
    (C) A new action movie
    (D) A new streaming-service drama

14. According to the article, what is one of the recent Netmovies' goals?
    (A) To attract the most popular actors
    (B) To get new customers
    (C) To buy more original stories
    (D) To increase its stock price

15. Which of the following is an error made by Hollywood Today in their article?
    (A) The numbers of languages and books sold were mistakenly switched.
    (B) Netmovies has plans to produce its own content in the future.
    (C) The actor's name has been misspelled.
    (D) *The Queen's Crown* is produced by a different company.

16. What did Ms. Forester mention in her e-mail?
    (A) The show title will have a different title from the book.
    (B) Netmovies is producing a show.
    (C) Netmovies published the book.
    (D) Dream Forever is a division of Netmovies Inc.

17. In which of the positions marked [1], [2], [3], and [4] does the following sentence best belong?
   "We would appreciate it if you could correct this as well."
    (A) [1]
    (B) [2]
    (C) [3]
    (D) [4]

▶Incomplete Sentences as REVIEW TEST

Part 5 Select the best choice to complete the sentence.

18. The ------- date for submitting the rough copy is next Monday.
(A) dead
(B) due
(C) closing
(D) finishing

19. The radio station aired a ------- ad for the upcoming concert to attract more attendees.
(A) promotionally
(B) promote
(C) promotional
(D) promotion

20. Users can ------- our service to gain unlimited access to a vast library of movies.
(A) subscribe to
(B) subscribe
(C) subscribe for
(D) subscribe in

21. The online retailer ------- an advertisement on a popular e-commerce website.
(A) placed
(B) published
(C) invested
(D) increased

22. The company posted an announcement ------- their official website.
(A) by
(B) at
(C) in
(D) on

23. The company will ------- out press releases to media outlets.
(A) figure
(B) carry
(C) send
(D) work

24. The editor-in-chief, ------- has vast experience in the industry, knows best how to guide the team.
(A) whoever
(B) anyone
(C) which
(D) who

健康

健康に関する問題は、近年その関心の高まりから必ず出題されています。健康診断から食事、運動、睡眠に関する設問はもちろん、病院（歯科、眼科、内科、外科など）との連絡や、医師や看護師との会話など出題パターンに慣れておきましょう。

> ## TOEIC® L&R頻出ボキャブラリーチェック

▶病気に関する表現 　🔊 Audio ① 46

1. One common _____ of the flu is a fever.
   インフルエンザの一般的な症状のひとつは発熱です。

2. Early detection and treatment are _____ in managing many _____.
   多くの病気において早期発見と治療が重要です。

3. High _____ _____ can lead to serious health problems.
   高血圧は深刻な健康問題につながる可能性があります。

4. Changes in appetite or weight can be _____ of stress.
   食欲や体重の変化はストレスのサインである可能性があります。

▶病院・薬局での表現

5. I need to _____ _____ _____ with my doctor.
   私は主治医に予約を取る必要があります。

6. The _____ explained how to take my _____ tablets.
   薬剤師は処方箋薬の飲み方を説明してくれました。

7. I stopped by the _____ to pick up some _____ medicine.
   私は咳止めを取りに薬局に立ち寄りました。

▶健康全般について

8. Eating a balanced _____ is essential for getting proper _____.
   栄養をきちんと摂るためにはバランスの良い食事をすることが大切です。

9. I have _____ a _____ with my dentist for next week.
   私は来週歯科検診を予定しています。

10. Walking is also an _____ activity for improving mental well-being.
    ウォーキングは、精神の健康を向上させるのにも適した活動です。

Listening Parts

≫ Photographs 🔊 Audio ① 47-48

Part 1 Please listen to four statements about a photograph. When you hear the statements, you must select one statement from (A), (B), (C), or (D) that best describes the photograph.

1. Ⓐ Ⓑ Ⓒ Ⓓ

2. Ⓐ Ⓑ Ⓒ Ⓓ

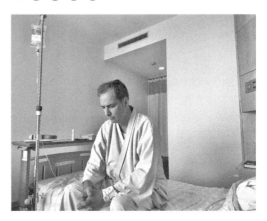

≫ Question-Response 🔊 Audio ① 49-50

Part 2 Please listen to a question or statement and three responses spoken in English. Then, choose the best response to the question or statement from (A), (B), or (C).

3. Ⓐ Ⓑ Ⓒ
4. Ⓐ Ⓑ Ⓒ
5. Ⓐ Ⓑ Ⓒ
6. Ⓐ Ⓑ Ⓒ

>> Short Conversations 🔊 Audio ① 51-53

Part 3 Please listen to a short conversation between two or more people. You must listen carefully to understand what the speakers say. You are to choose the best answer to each question.

7. What is the woman's current physical condition?
   (A) She has a persistent fever.
   (B) She has a cough and a headache.
   (C) She has a bad stomachache.
   (D) She has a backache.

8. How long has the woman had these symptoms?
   (A) Three days   (C) Ten days
   (B) Seven days   (D) Thirty days

9. What tests does the man recommend for the woman?
   (A) A blood test and a urine test   (C) A blood test and a chest X-ray
   (B) A chest X-ray and a urine test   (D) A blood test and a CT scan

>> Short Talks 🔊 Audio ① 54-56

Part 4 Please listen to a short talk. You must listen carefully to understand and remember what is said. You are to choose the best answer to each question.

10. According to the speaker, why is mental health important?
    (A) It affects our physical health.
    (B) It affects our feelings and actions.
    (C) It affects our significant other's well-being.
    (D) It affects our ability to budget money well.

11. What are some factors that can impact our mental health?
    (A) Exercise and meditation   (C) Diet and sleep
    (B) Stress, trauma, and genetics   (D) Social media and technology

12. What will the participants do next?
    (A) They will conduct a self-check on their mental health.
    (B) They will apply for a mental health course to learn coping skills.
    (C) They will begin exercising outdoors to improve their mental health.
    (D) They will schedule an appointment to see a doctor for further evaluation.

Unit

5

健
康

>> Reading Comprehension

Part 7 Choose the best answer, (A), (B), (C), or (D), to each question.

Questions 13-17 refer to the following article, schedule, and e-mail.

"The Benefits of Regular Exercise"

Regular exercise is an essential part of a healthy lifestyle. It can help to reduce the risk of chronic diseases such as diabetes, heart disease, and cancer. Exercise can also improve mental health and well-being, reducing stress and anxiety levels. However, it is important to exercise safely and to choose activities that are appropriate for your fitness level and health status. Start exercising today to see benefits within as little as one week.

Jupiter GYM
Kickboxing Schedule

	Monday	Tuesday	Wednesday	Thursday	Friday	Saturday	Sunday
12 P.M.-1 P.M.						Beginners	
3 P.M.-4 P.M.							Advanced
4 P.M.-5 P.M.					Advanced		
5 P.M.-6 P.M.						Beginners	Beginners
6 P.M.-7 P.M.						Advanced	Advanced
7 P.M.-8 P.M.	Beginners	Advanced	Beginners				Beginners
8 P.M.-9 P.M.	Advanced	Advanced	Advanced		Advanced		

To: marybrowne77@geemail.com
From: samanthayoung72@geemail.com
Date: May 12
Subject: Thanks

Hey Mary,

To answer your question, our meeting has been changed to tomorrow afternoon. Double-check with Frank when you get to the office tomorrow about the new location.

Oh, also thanks for forwarding me that article. It was the kick I needed. I did some homework and found the Jupiter Gym schedule online, and it looks like there'll be at least one suitable time for me. I've never done this before, so I'm a little nervous. You said you go to the last class on Tuesdays, so I don't think we'll see each other. I only have time on the weekends in the early afternoon. Can once a week be considered regular exercise? Well, I have to begin somewhere. Wish me luck!

See you tomorrow,
Sam

13. What is one benefit of regular exercise mentioned in the article?
    (A) To defend yourself in dangerous situations
    (B) To increase chances to meet new people
    (C) To improve mental health
    (D) To completely avoid diseases like cancer and heart disease

14. What most likely is the relationship between Mary and Sam?
    (A) Work colleagues   (C) Gym instructor and student
    (B) Gym friends   (D) School classmates

15. What kickboxing class does Mary attend?
    (A) Beginners 12 P.M.-1 P.M.
    (B) Beginners 7 P.M.-8 P.M.
    (C) Advanced 4 P.M.-5 P.M.
    (D) Advanced 8 P.M.-9 P.M.

16. What kickboxing class will Sam most likely take?
    (A) Tuesday Advanced 8 P.M.-9 P.M.
    (B) Wednesday Beginners 7 P.M.-8 P.M.
    (C) Saturday Beginners 12 P.M.-1 P.M.
    (D) Sunday Advanced 3 P.M.-4 P.M.

17. In the e-mail, the word "kick" in paragraph 2, line 1, is closest in meaning to
    (A) instruction   (C) hope
    (B) motivation   (D) desire

▶ Incomplete Sentences as REVIEW TEST

Part 5 Select the best choice to complete the sentence.

18. It is important to ------- an appointment with the dentist every six months.
    (A) call
    (C) make
    (B) carry
    (D) take

19. One of the ------- gave me advice on which medication to take for my cold.
    (A) pharmaceutical
    (C) pharmaceuticals
    (B) pharmacies
    (D) pharmacists

20. ------- experiencing several symptoms, she refused to go to the doctor.
    (A) Although
    (C) Despite
    (B) When
    (D) Due to

21. Taking the ------- medication at the right time is critical for a sick person to recover faster.
    (A) prescribed
    (C) prescription
    (B) prescribing
    (D) prescribe

22. Regular exercise is a ------- factor in physical health.
    (A) crucial
    (C) severe
    (B) precious
    (D) meaningful

23. A diet that ------- a variety of nutrients can provide energy.
    (A) is included
    (C) to include
    (B) includes
    (D) include

24. Getting an ------- amount of sleep is essential for maintaining good physical health.
    (A) extra
    (C) advanced
    (B) appropriate
    (D) accurate

旅行 ②

TOEIC® L&Rでは、旅行に関する問題がよく出題されます。ホテルや施設、旅行代理店の案内、宿泊先とのメールのやりとりなどのパターンがありますので、旅行に関する表現に慣れておくとよいでしょう。

>> **TOEIC® L&R頻出ボキャブラリーチェック**

▶電車や飛行機、バスなどの移動手段に関する表現 🔊 Audio ① 57

1. There are several _____ options available in this city.
   この街にはいくつかの交通手段があります。

2. Your flight has been delayed due to the _____ weather.
   悪天候のため飛行機が遅れております。

3. Do you offer any discounts for booking a _____ _____?
   往復予約すると割引はありますか？

4. Are there any _____ _____ available for this train?
   この列車に通路側の空席はありますか？

▶観光に関する表現

5. Could you give me a _____ that includes a map of the city's landmarks?
   市の名所の地図が掲載されているパンフレットをいただけますか。

6. One of the best ways to _____ this city is to take a walking tour.
   この街を散策するのに最適な方法のひとつは、ウォーキングツアーへの参加です。

7. The hotel is located _____ _____ _____ of the city's main attractions.
   ホテルは市内の主要な観光スポットから徒歩圏内に位置しています。

8. A: Who wants to join this tour with me? B: _____ _____ _____!
   A: 誰か私とこのツアーに参加しない？ B: 私も参加させて！

9. Our team _____ _____ _____ _____ you around the city.
   私たちのチームは市内を案内するのを楽しみにしています。

▶旅行会社や代理店との会話

10. Can you provide us with a list of _____ _____ in the area?
    この地域にある手頃な宿泊施設を教えてください。

11. We invite you to _____ _____ _____ _____.
    アンケートへのご記入をお願いしています。

12. Before you depart, make sure to _____ _____ _____.
    出発する前に、必ず予約を確認してください。

Listening Parts

>> Photographs 📶 Audio ① 58-59

Part 1 Please listen to four statements about a photograph. When you hear the statements, you must select one statement from (A), (B), (C), or (D) that best describes the photograph.

1. Ⓐ Ⓑ Ⓒ Ⓓ

2. Ⓐ Ⓑ Ⓒ Ⓓ

>> Question-Response 📶 Audio ① 60-61

Part 2 Please listen to a question or statement and three responses spoken in English. Then, choose the best response to the question or statement from (A), (B), or (C).

3. Ⓐ Ⓑ Ⓒ
4. Ⓐ Ⓑ Ⓒ
5. Ⓐ Ⓑ Ⓒ
6. Ⓐ Ⓑ Ⓒ

>> Short Conversations 🔊 Audio ① 62-64

Part 3 Please listen to a short conversation between two or more people. You must listen carefully to understand what the speakers say. You are to choose the best answer to each question.

7. What is the woman doing?
   (A) Hiking
   (B) Eating
   (C) Sightseeing
   (D) Snowboarding

8. How will the woman most likely visit the museum?
   (A) By bus
   (B) On foot
   (C) By taxi
   (D) By train

9. What type of restaurant does the man recommend?
   (A) A vegetarian restaurant
   (B) A reasonable restaurant
   (C) An eclectic restaurant
   (D) An exclusive restaurant

>> Short Talks 🔊 Audio ① 65-67

Part 4 Please listen to a short talk. You must listen carefully to understand and remember what is said. You are to choose the best answer to each question.

10. Which station comes after Newark?
    (A) Elizabeth
    (B) Trenton
    (C) Philadelphia
    (D) Princeton

11. Where should passengers change trains if they want to go to Princeton?
    (A) Newark
    (B) Trenton
    (C) Jersey City
    (D) Princeton Junction

12. Why is the replacement bus service in operation?
    (A) Due to inclement weather
    (B) Due to engineering work
    (C) Due to an accident
    (D) Due to signal trouble

>> Reading Comprehension

Part 7 Choose the best answer, (A), (B), (C), or (D), to each question.

Questions 13-15 refer to the following e-mail.

To: Hina Yamaguchi
From: Charles Blare
Date: April 15
Subject: Online survey
Attachment: 🔗Brochure for this summer

Dear Ms. Hina Yamaguchi,

Thank you for giving Pacific Travel Inc. the opportunity to make your travel arrangements for your recent trip to the Gold Coast in Australia.

We sincerely hope that you were pleased with the air travel and the accommodations last month that we arranged for you. We encourage you to leave comments on our online customer satisfaction survey, as it is the best means for learning firsthand of ways to better serve our valued customers like you in the future.

We will look forward to helping you again for your next vacation or business trip. Thank you.

Yours truly,

Charles Blare

---

13. Why did Mr. Blare send his e-mail to Ms. Yamaguchi?
   (A) To accept her sincere apologies
   (B) To ask her to fill in a survey
   (C) To confirm her reservation
   (D) To recommend another destination

14. When did Ms. Yamaguchi travel to Australia?
   (A) March   (C) May
   (B) April   (D) August

15. What is sent together with this e-mail?

(A) An invoice

(B) An itinerary

(C) A pamphlet

(D) A refund check

Questions 16-18 refer to the following article.

Traveling is a popular way to explore the world and gain new experiences. Whether it's for business or pleasure, traveling allows you to immerse yourself in new cultures, try new foods, and meet new people.

When planning a trip, it's important to consider transportation options. Air travel is often the fastest and most convenient way to travel long distances. However, it can be expensive and may involve long waits at airports. Train travel is a comfortable and scenic option but may be slower and less efficient for long distances. Bus travel is often the most affordable choice but can be uncomfortable for long periods.

No matter how you choose to travel, planning ahead and researching your options can help ensure a smooth and enjoyable trip.

16. What is mentioned about air travel?

(A) It offers the most scenic experience.

(B) It is usually the most affordable option.

(C) It offers a comfortable and stress-free way to travel.

(D) It is the best way to travel a considerable distance.

17. The word "immerse" in paragraph 1, line 2, is closest in meaning to

(A) find

(B) dive

(C) adapt

(D) change

18. What is recommended for readers?

(A) To budget travel costs

(B) To select the best hotel

(C) To make arrangements in advance

(D) To consult a travel agent

Incomplete Sentences as REVIEW TEST

Part 5 Select the best choice to complete the sentence.

19. The train station was ------- walking distance of our hostel.
(A) during
(B) within
(C) along
(D) beyond

20. We are all looking forward to ------- on the beach in Hawaii.
(A) relaxed
(B) relax
(C) relaxing
(D) being relaxed

21. We rented a car to ------- the countryside and see the natural beauty of this region.
(A) explore
(B) wander
(C) transport
(D) immerse

22. The hiking trail was closed ------- the inclement weather and won't be open again until conditions improve.
(A) in case of
(B) due to
(C) because
(D) since

23. You will receive a ------- e-mail after you make your reservation.
(A) confirmed
(B) confirmative
(C) confirming
(D) confirmation

24. The hotel can ------- up to 200 guests for a conference or event in its ballroom.
(A) stay
(B) offer
(C) accommodate
(D) reserve

25. The car rental company offers ------- rates for long-term rentals.
(A) affording
(B) afford
(C) affordably
(D) affordable

オフィス ②

TOEIC® L&Rで設問に使われるトピックスは、ビジネスにおける状況 (business settings) に関連していることが多いです。したがって、オフィスでの従業員同士の会話表現、社内の業務連絡 (memorandum)、内外へのオンラインチャット (text-message chain) での連絡などに関する表現に慣れておきましょう。

≫ TOEIC® L&R頻出ボキャブラリーチェック

▶同僚との会話 🔊 Audio ① 68

1. Please _____ all necessary documents with your slides so we can _____ review them.
   必要な書類をスライドに同封してください、そうすれば迅速に検討することができます。

2. We increased our _____ levels based on the projected _____ _____.
   予測売上高に基づいて、在庫量を増やしました。

3. Would you be able to provide an _____ report for this _____?
   今期の在庫報告書をいただけますか？

4. Have you prepared your presentation for the _____ client meeting?
   今度の顧客との打ち合わせに向けたプレゼンの準備はできましたか？

▶人事評価について

5. It's important to listen to the _____ of our _____.
   同僚の懸念に耳を傾けることは重要です。

6. We'd like to _____ your _____ _____ the success of the project.
   プロジェクトの成功のために尽力してくれた功績を称えたいと思います。

7. We _____ your _____ _____ the team and your hard work.
   チームへの貢献とあなたの頑張りに感謝します。

▶顧客とのやり取り

8. _____ you will find the _____ outlining our agreement.
   添付の契約書は、私たちの合意の概要です。

9. Our _____ equipment will _____ the quality of your products.
   当社の最新鋭の機器によって、お客様の製品の品質がさらに向上します。

10. To _____ _____ _____, simply reply to this e-mail.
    ご注文の際は、このメールにご返信ください。

11. Please _____ _____ _____ _____ me if you have any questions.
    ご質問等ございましたら、遠慮なくご連絡ください。

12. Our _____ _____ will be in touch with you shortly to discuss the details.
    弊社営業担当が詳細を追ってご連絡いたします。

>> Photographs 🔊 Audio ① 69-70

Part 1 Please listen to four statements about a photograph. When you hear the statements, you must select one statement from (A), (B), (C), or (D) that best describes the photograph.

1. Ⓐ Ⓑ Ⓒ Ⓓ

2. Ⓐ Ⓑ Ⓒ Ⓓ

>> Question-Response 🔊 Audio ① 71-72

Part 2 Please listen to a question or statement and three responses spoken in English. Then, choose the best response to the question or statement from (A), (B), or (C).

3. Ⓐ Ⓑ Ⓒ
4. Ⓐ Ⓑ Ⓒ
5. Ⓐ Ⓑ Ⓒ
6. Ⓐ Ⓑ Ⓒ

≫ Short Conversations 🔊 Audio ① 73-75

Part 3 Please listen to a short conversation between two or more people. You must listen carefully to understand what the speakers say. You are to choose the best answer to each question.

7. What is the woman inquiring about?
(A) Stationery stock
(B) Sales figures
(C) Customer service
(D) Marketing campaign posters

8. How many blue pens does the office have?
(A) 100
(B) 200
(C) 300
(D) 500

9. Who most likely are the speakers?
(A) A boss and a subordinate
(B) Old friends
(C) A customer and a sales representative
(D) Office colleagues

≫ Short Talks 🔊 Audio ① 76-78

Part 4 Please listen to a short talk. You must listen carefully to understand and remember what is said. You are to choose the best answer to each question.

10. What is the purpose of this telephone message?
(A) To confirm the production schedule
(B) To remind someone of a factory visit
(C) To inform of a schedule change
(D) To warn about safety regulations

11. What will be showcased during the visit?
(A) The company's history
(B) The factory's employees
(C) The latest products
(D) The company's wearable shoes

12. What are the listeners asked to wear during the factory tour?
(A) Closed-toe shoes
(B) Security hats
(C) Eyeglasses
(D) Special clothing

>> Text Completion

Part 6 Select the best choice to complete the text.

Questions 13-16 refer to the following e-mail.

To: All Employees
From: Nancy Kim
Date: April 23
Subject: Performance Evaluation Process

It's that time of year again! Our performance evaluation process ------, and we
13.
encourage everyone to take this opportunity to reflect on their achievements
and identify areas for improvement. The process will consist of three steps:
self-assessment, manager evaluation, and performance discussion. ------.
14.
To start the process, we ask that you ------ writing your self-assessment. This
15.
is your chance to reflect on your performance and set goals for the future.

We appreciate your dedication ------ our company and your own professional
16.
growth. If you have any questions, please don't hesitate to reach out to your
manager or HR representative.

Nancy Kim
Human Resources Director

---

13. (A) will have started
    (B) to start
    (C) is starting
    (D) had started

14. (A) Please take this process seriously and provide
       thoughtful feedback.
    (B) Think carefully about what you need to purchase
       and when.
    (C) It is time to get a little creative and make a few
       changes.
    (D) You can work on morale and ensure that team
       spirit is alive.

15. (A) schedule
    (B) begin
    (C) determine
    (D) create

16. (A) with
    (B) to
    (C) on
    (D) of

>> Reading Comprehension

Part 7 Choose the best answer, (A), (B), (C), or (D), to each question.

Questions 17-18 refer to the following text-message chain.

Unit

7

オフィス②

> **Jeff Savage 7:31 A.M.**
> Hey, Clare. Forgot my work ID card. Could you let the entrance security guards know to let me in? I'm almost at the office and don't have time to go back to my house.

> **Clare Smith 7:33 A.M.**
> I've come down with something so won't be around today. I'll message Kathy right now.

> **Jeff Savage 7:37 A.M.**
> Sorry to hear about your situation. Don't worry, I'll ask Kathy.

> **Clare Smith 7:40 A.M.**
> OK. Thanks. It's not serious. I'll probably see you tomorrow!

> **Jeff Savage 7:42 A.M.**
> Great. Take care!

17. What happened to Mr. Savage?
 (A) He will be late for work.
 (B) He cannot find his wallet.
 (C) His work identification is at home.
 (D) He has lost his phone.

18. At 7:40 A.M., what does Ms. Smith mean when she writes, "It's not serious."?
 (A) Asking Kathy is no trouble.
 (B) Asking the guards is no trouble.
 (C) She should be feeling OK soon.
 (D) Being absent from work is no problem.

Incomplete Sentences as REVIEW TEST

Part 5 Select the best choice to complete the sentence.

19. We are ------- a gift as a token of our appreciation for your continued support.
(A) enclosing
(B) applying
(C) carrying
(D) redeeming

20. The manager acted ------- to resolve the issue and prevent any further complications.
(A) prompt
(B) promptness
(C) promptly
(D) prompting

21. The company wishes to ------- your outstanding work.
(A) contribute
(B) recognize
(C) achieve
(D) undergo

22. Productivity has improved ------- we started working with state-of-the-art tools.
(A) therefore
(B) although
(C) besides
(D) since

23. We understand the ------- of our customers and are addressing them swiftly.
(A) status
(B) challenges
(C) concerns
(D) assignments

24. Our company has created a ------- website for our new product launch.
(A) dedicated
(B) dedicating
(C) dedication
(D) delicately

25. Our company is excited to announce the ------- launch of our product line next month.
(A) whole
(B) upcoming
(C) severe
(D) once

不動産・住宅 ────────────

TOEIC® L&Rでは、不動産や住宅に関する設問がよく出題されます。米国人は生涯における転居回数が日本人と比較しても多く、引っ越しやそれに伴う住宅探し、修繕作業、不動産の売買は生活の一部と言ってもよいでしょう。

>> ## TOEIC® L&R頻出ボキャブラリーチェック

▶住宅の改修・修理で頻出の表現　📶 Audio ① 79

1. We apologize for the _____, but our building is currently _____ _____.
   ご不便をおかけしております、建物は現在工事中となっております。

2. To prevent further issues, _____ _____ the sink and _____ _____ _____.
   更なる問題を防ぐため、流しの使用を避け排水管を修理してください。

3. The _____ came to check the _____ to ensure they were installed correctly.
   検査員が窓ガラスが正しく取り付けられているか確認しに来ました。

4. The _____ has to provide _____ for the doorway.
   入居者はドアの寸法を提示しなければなりません。

▶不動産屋との会話

5. We specialize in _____ _____ _____ for short-term leases.
   当社は短期賃貸の家具付き不動産に特化しております。

6. We provide the rental place that will _____ client's needs and budget.
   お客様のご要望やご予算に合わせて、賃貸物件をご提案いたします。

7. We have _____ studio apartments _____ one-bedroom apartments available for rent.
   当社はワンルーム、または1ベッドルームをご用意しております。

8. This space is _____ _____ out if you're looking for a location to start your business.
   起業のための場所をお探しでしたら、このスペースはご覧いただく価値があります。

9. I'd _____ _____ _____ help you find the perfect _____.
   喜んでお客様の理想の物件探しのお手伝いをさせていただきます。

10. Please _____ _____ _____ take a virtual tour of our apartments on our website.
    当社ホームページでのお部屋のバーチャルツアーをどうぞお気軽にご利用ください。

≫ Photographs 📶 Audio ① 80-81

Part 1   Please listen to four statements about a photograph. When you hear the statements, you must select one statement from (A), (B), (C), or (D) that best describes the photograph.

1. Ⓐ Ⓑ Ⓒ Ⓓ

2. Ⓐ Ⓑ Ⓒ Ⓓ

≫ Question-Response 📶 Audio ① 82-83

Part 2   Please listen to a question or statement and three responses spoken in English. Then, choose the best response to the question or statement from (A), (B), or (C).

3. Ⓐ Ⓑ Ⓒ
4. Ⓐ Ⓑ Ⓒ
5. Ⓐ Ⓑ Ⓒ
6. Ⓐ Ⓑ Ⓒ

>> Short Conversations 🔊 Audio ① 84-86

Part 3 Please listen to a short conversation between two or more people. You must listen carefully to understand what the speakers say. You are to choose the best answer to each question.

7. What is the woman's problem?
   (A) Her kitchen is too small.
   (B) Her bathroom is flooded.
   (C) Her water pipes are blocked.
   (D) Her room is cluttered.

8. What does the woman ask the man to do?
   (A) To fix it when it's convenient for him
   (B) To come to her home by himself
   (C) To send someone today
   (D) To let her use his shower

9. What will the man most likely do next?
   (A) Contact a maintenance team
   (B) Complete an inspection report
   (C) Rent a different room
   (D) Send a payment bill

>> Short Talks 🔊 Audio ① 87-89

Part 4 Please listen to a short talk. You must listen carefully to understand and remember what is said. You are to choose the best answer to each question.

10. Where most likely does the speaker work?
    (A) At a car rental agency
    (B) At a real estate agency
    (C) At a bicycle shop
    (D) At a shopping center

11. What is suggested about the listener from this message?
    (A) She is an international student.
    (B) She does not have a driver's license.
    (C) She does not have a car.
    (D) She will commute by bicycle.

12. What can the listener choose?
    (A) Larger or smaller rooms
    (B) Reasonable or luxurious rooms
    (C) Furnished or unfurnished rooms
    (D) East side or west side rooms

Unit

8

不動産・住宅

» Reading Comprehension

Part 7 Choose the best answer, (A), (B), (C), or (D), to each question.

Questions 13-15 refer to the following advertisement.

Dear potential renters,

We are excited to announce the availability of our newly renovated apartment complex, located in the heart of the city, for rental to newly coming families. Our spacious and modern apartments are designed to offer a comfortable and convenient living experience, perfect for those seeking a cozy home in the city.

Our apartments come equipped with all the necessary amenities, including air conditioning, heating, modern kitchen appliances, and in-unit laundry facilities. Additionally, our community offers a range of features to make your living experience even more enjoyable, such as a fitness center, swimming pool, and on-site management team.

At our complex, we understand the importance of family and the need for a secure living environment. That's why we offer a gated community, surveillance cameras throughout the property, and a professional security team on-site 24/7.

If you're looking for a comfortable and convenient place to call home, our apartments are the perfect fit for you and your family. Contact us today to schedule a tour and learn more about our leasing options.

---

13. What is the purpose of this advertisement?
(A) To recruit renters
(B) To promote new amenities
(C) To schedule a tour
(D) To contact residents

14. What is NOT true about the apartment complex?
(A) It is newly constructed.
(B) It has a fitness gym.
(C) It is furnished with modern kitchen appliances.
(D) It offers an in-unit laundry.

15. What is indicated about the security system?
   (A) Surveillance cameras will be installed.
   (B) Baggage screening is conducted.
   (C) A security team is always on duty.
   (D) Motion detectors are activated at night.

Questions 16-18 refer to the following letter.

Subject: Moving Sale: Get Exciting Discounts on Our High-Quality Products!

I am writing to let you know that I am moving to a new house soon and I have decided to organize a moving sale. The sale will feature a variety of high-quality items, including furniture, electronics, kitchenware, and decorative pieces, all in excellent condition. All the products will be available at discounted prices, and I assure you that the items are worth checking out.

Here are some of the products that will be on sale.

• Sofa sets, dining tables, and chairs
• LED TVs, home theater systems, and gaming consoles
• Kitchen appliances, including blenders, juicers, and microwave ovens
• Decorative pieces, including lamps, paintings, and vases

The moving sale will be held on June 4th, next Saturday, at my current residence, which is located in room #802. The sale will start at 10:00 A.M. and will continue until 5:00 P.M. I would be delighted if you could stop by and have a look at the products.

Please feel free to share this e-mail with your family and friends who might be interested in purchasing some quality items at discounted prices.

Thank you for your time and consideration, and I hope to see you at the moving sale.

Best regards,
Tom Stevens

---

16. Which items will be available for sale?
   (A) Fruits and vegetables
   (B) Stationery items
   (C) Household goods
   (D) Clothes and accessories

17. What is mentioned about Mr. Stevens?
   (A) He is running a furniture store.
   (B) He is changing his address.
   (C) He is traveling abroad.
   (D) He is remodeling his room.

18. Where will the moving sale take place?
   (A) At the recipient's house
   (B) At the sender's new house
   (C) At the sender's current house
   (D) At a public park

▶ Incomplete Sentences as REVIEW TEST

Part 5 Select the best choice to complete the sentence.

19. The house we are looking at is available for rent and comes fully -------.
   (A) furnish
   (B) furniture
   (C) furnishing
   (D) furnished

20. The property features multiple bedrooms to ------- a growing family.
   (A) adopt
   (B) accommodate
   (C) fill
   (D) meet

21. It is crucial to avoid ------- faulty electrical wiring or outdated electrical equipment.
   (A) using
   (B) to use
   (C) use
   (D) usage

22. The plumber needed the ------- of the pipes to fix the plumbing issue.
(A) meters
(B) quantities
(C) measurements
(D) volumes

23. The majority of real estate companies invest in either residential ------- commercial real estate.
(A) or
(B) and
(C) nor
(D) but

24. The electrical system underwent ------- by a qualified electrician.
(A) inspectional
(B) inspect
(C) inspector
(D) inspection

25. This building is temporarily closed to the public as it is currently ------- construction.
(A) due to
(B) under
(C) by
(D) during

ショッピング

TOEIC® L&Rでは、ショッピングに関する設問が出題されます。衣料品店や書店での
やりとり、不良品 (defective product) に対する消費者からの交換 (replacement) や
返金 (refund) のリクエストなど、様々な場面が出題されます。

>> TOEIC® L&R頻出ボキャブラリーチェック

▶店員との会話 🔊 Audio ② 01

1. A: Do you have the new gaming console _____ _____?
   A: 新しいゲーム機の在庫はありますか？

   B: Sorry, but we're currently _____ _____ _____.
   B: 申し訳ございませんが、現在在庫がありません。

2. A: Excuse me, I'd like to _____ about the _____ of this item in size M.
   A: すみません、この商品のMサイズの在庫状況をお伺いしたいのですが。

   B: Certainly! Let me check our _____ for you.
   B: 承知いたしました！　在庫を確認して参ります。

▶買い物に関連する情報を伝える表現

3. Our _____ covers any defects or malfunctions and is provided _____
   _____ _____.

   当店の保証はいかなる欠陥や故障も対象となり、無償で提供されます。

4. Our shop _____ our _____ _____, offering special _____.
   当店ではロイヤリティ・プログラムに力を入れており、特別な特典がございます。

5. Upon receiving your order, we will send you an _____ including the _____
   _____.

   ご注文いただき次第、送料込みの請求書をお送りいたします。

6. For _____ _____ _____, please visit our store with the receipts and
   _____ _____.

   現金での返金をご希望の場合は、レシートと連絡先をお持ちの上ご来店ください。

▶販売業務に関する表現

7. _____ support _____ with _____ options for product issues.
   卸売業者は製品の問題のための交換オプションで小売業者をサポートします。

8. Based on the _____ demand, we _____ the featured products.
   需要予測に基づき、当店では目玉商品を陳列しています。

▶ Listening Parts

≫ Photographs 🔊 Audio② 02-03

Part 1 Please listen to four statements about a photograph. When you hear the statements, you must select one statement from (A), (B), (C), or (D) that best describes the photograph.

1. Ⓐ Ⓑ Ⓒ Ⓓ

2. Ⓐ Ⓑ Ⓒ Ⓓ

≫ Question-Response 🔊 Audio② 04-05

Part 2 Please listen to a question or statement and three responses spoken in English. Then, choose the best response to the question or statement from (A), (B), or (C).

3. Ⓐ Ⓑ Ⓒ
4. Ⓐ Ⓑ Ⓒ
5. Ⓐ Ⓑ Ⓒ
6. Ⓐ Ⓑ Ⓒ

>> Short Conversations 🔊 Audio ② 06-08

7. Where most likely does the conversation take place?
   (A) At a shoe shop   (C) At a manufacturer
   (B) At a theater ticket counter   (D) At a warehouse

8. What does the man ask the woman to do?
   (A) Find a product   (C) Reduce the price
   (B) Buy shoes   (D) Repair the rack

9. What will the man do next?
   (A) He will wait for a while.
   (B) He will try to find his shoes.
   (C) He will go to another store.
   (D) He will take off his shoes.

>> Short Talks 🔊 Audio ② 09-11

10. What is D-Mart Stores?
    (A) A manufacturer   (C) A retailer
    (B) A wholesaler   (D) An Internet service provider

11. According to the speaker, what is the problem with the company?
    (A) It mistakenly reported its market share.
    (B) It lost trust among its customers.
    (C) It could not launch a national TV ad campaign.
    (D) It was predicted to go bankrupt.

12. What will D-Mart do soon?
    (A) They will launch a new outlet.
    (B) They will adopt a price match policy.
    (C) They will reverse its merchandising policy.
    (D) They will renew its facilities.

Reading Parts

>> Reading Comprehension

Part 7 Choose the best answer, (A), (B), (C), or (D), to each question.

Questions 13-17 refer to the following e-mail and invoice.

To: customerservices@sunnydays.com
From: tedbranson@geemail.com
Subject: Order on June 15
Date: June 29

To whom it may concern,

I ordered something from your company on June 15th. When I got the order, I realized that one of the items I ordered was delivered in the wrong size. I wanted an XL size, but it says L on the item. The invoice also confirms the correct size I ordered so there must have been some mistake. I often order things from your website, but this is the first time I've received the incorrect item. This is a birthday present so I would need the correct size soon. Can you please tell me how to best proceed?

Awaiting your reply,
Ted Branson

Sunny Days Clothing Company

Order No: WZ5GH2   **June 16**

Quantity	Size	Item	Price
1	L	Men's T-shirt blue (mt389b)	$20.00
1	L	Men's T-shirt green (mt389g)	$15.00
1	XL	Men's dress shirt white (mds778w)	$40.00
1	M	Kid's T-shirt blue (kt333b)	$25.00
1	M	Kid's T-shirt green (kt333g)	$22.00

Subtotal: $122.00
Tax: $12.20
Coupon: -$20.00
Shipping: $10.00
Total: $124.20

Paid by: *North American Express XXXX XXXXXX* 3789
Order inquiries should be directed at: customerservices@sunnydays.com

13. What is the purpose of Mr. Branson's e-mail?
(A) To explain a mistake with an order
(B) To describe a problem he had with the website
(C) To ask a question about clothing inventory
(D) To disagree with the company's policy

14. What can be inferred about Mr. Branson from the e-mail?
(A) He is celebrating his birthday soon.
(B) He works for Sunny Days Clothing Company.
(C) He has ordered from the company before.
(D) He would like the company to call him.

15. What is the price of the item Mr. Branson did not receive?
(A) $15.00
(B) $20.00
(C) $25.00
(D) $40.00

16. What does the invoice indicate about the order?
(A) It was shipped free of charge.
(B) It included women's clothing.
(C) It had a discount applied.
(D) It was paid in cash.

17. What information can be found on the invoice?
(A) Mr. Branson's address
(B) Information on how to return items
(C) Company contact information
(D) The company's website address

▶Incomplete Sentences as REVIEW TEST

Part 5 Select the best choice to complete the sentence.

18. The item that was previously out of stock is now back ------- stock.
    (A) on
    (B) at
    (C) in
    (D) of

19. The customer visited the store and ------- about the return policy for a defective item.
    (A) inquiring
    (B) to inquire
    (C) inquiries
    (D) inquired

20. The manager diligently keeps track of the ------- to ensure accurate stock levels.
    (A) inventory
    (B) remains
    (C) routine
    (D) leftovers

21. The sales forecast ------- a 20% increase in sales during the holiday season.
    (A) predicted
    (B) was predicted
    (C) predicting
    (D) predict

22. ------- you paid in cash, please visit our customer service desk for assistance with your refund.
    (A) Although
    (B) If
    (C) Upon
    (D) Since

23. We may use the ------- information you provide to send you promotional offers.
    (A) contacting
    (B) contact
    (C) contacted
    (D) contactable

24. The credit card offers attractive ------- such as airline miles or cash-back.
    (A) refunds
    (B) reimbursement
    (C) rewards
    (D) receipts

TOEIC® L&Rでは、職位の空き（job openings）、面接試験（job interview）、求人広告（classified ad）、照会状（a letter of reference）、履歴書（résumé, CV）、採用に関するレターやEメールなど、就職活動に関連した問題がほぼ毎回出題されます。

TOEIC® L&R頻出ボキャブラリーチェック

▶求人広告に頻出の表現 🔊 Audio ② 12

Job Title / Job Position: 職種

1. We are ＿＿＿＿＿ ＿＿＿＿＿ an ＿＿＿＿＿ Human Resource Administrator.
   当社では現在、人事総務の経験者を募集しています。

2. We are in search of a ＿＿＿＿＿ graphic designer.
   当社はグラフィックデザイナー（正社員）を募集しています。

Job ＿＿＿＿＿: 仕事内容・職務

3. Responsibilities ＿＿＿＿＿ ＿＿＿＿＿ ＿＿＿＿＿ customer inquiries.
   職務内容はお客様からのお問い合わせへの対応が含まれます。

Requirements / Qualifications: 応募条件・資格

4. Qualified ＿＿＿＿＿ must have at least three years of managerial ＿＿＿＿＿.
   条件を満たしている応募者は、管理職経験が少なくとも3年以上の方です。

5. We ＿＿＿＿＿ ＿＿＿＿＿ ＿＿＿＿＿ a candidate with the following ＿＿＿＿＿ :
   以下の資格をお持ちの方を募集しています：
   - A university ＿＿＿＿＿ in law　法律の学位をお持ちの方
   - Strong ＿＿＿＿＿ to join our team　当社のチームに参加する強い熱意がある方

Application Process: 応募方法

6. If you are interested in the ＿＿＿＿＿, please visit our website.
   このポジションに興味がおありの方は、当社のウェブサイトをご覧ください。

7. Please submit your ＿＿＿＿＿ and ＿＿＿＿＿ ＿＿＿＿＿ ＿＿＿＿＿ to the Personnel Department.　履歴書と紹介状を人事部までご提出ください。

8. In order to ＿＿＿＿＿ ＿＿＿＿＿ job-openings, you need to complete the ＿＿＿＿＿.　求人に応募するためには、登録が必要です。

▶求人応募メールに頻出の表現

9. I am ＿＿＿＿＿ in my ability to ＿＿＿＿＿ to your company's growth.
   私は御社の成長に貢献できる自信があります。

10. I have been ＿＿＿＿＿ for my ＿＿＿＿＿ sales performance.
    私はこれまで、優れた営業成績を評価されてきました。

Listening Parts

≫ Photographs 🔊 Audio② 13-14

Part 1 Please listen to four statements about a photograph. When you hear the statements, you must select one statement from (A), (B), (C), or (D) that best describes the photograph.

1. Ⓐ Ⓑ Ⓒ Ⓓ

2. Ⓐ Ⓑ Ⓒ Ⓓ

≫ Question-Response 🔊 Audio② 15-16

Part 2 Please listen to a question or statement and three responses spoken in English. Then, choose the best response to the question or statement from (A), (B), or (C).

3. Ⓐ Ⓑ Ⓒ
4. Ⓐ Ⓑ Ⓒ
5. Ⓐ Ⓑ Ⓒ
6. Ⓐ Ⓑ Ⓒ

>> Short Conversations 🔊 Audio ② 17-19

Part 3 Please listen to a short conversation between two or more people. You must listen carefully to understand what the speakers say. You are to choose the best answer to each question.

7. What will the man do tomorrow?
(A) He will attend an elementary school.　(C) He will have an interview.
(B) He will play with children.　(D) He will hire a teacher.

8. How is the man feeling?
(A) He is uneasy.　(C) He is irritated.
(B) He feels really relaxed.　(D) He is very confident.

9. What does the woman advise the man to do?
(A) To get a lot of sleep　(C) To show that he likes children
(B) To wear a suit　(D) To act like a child

>> Short Talks 🔊 Audio ② 20-22

Part 4 Please listen to a short talk. You must listen carefully to understand and remember what is said. You are to choose the best answer to each question.

10. Who most likely is the speaker?
(A) A trainer　(C) A recruiter
(B) An interviewer　(D) A job seeker

11. What does the speaker ask participants to do?
(A) To speak confidently
(B) To walk gracefully
(C) To avoid giving any bad impression
(D) To prepare a speech script

12. What will the participants do next?
(A) Make a public speech
(B) Take a pop quiz
(C) Have a practice interview
(D) Write about their goals

>> Reading Comprehension

Part 7 Choose the best answer, (A), (B), (C), or (D), to each question.

Questions 13-17 refer to the following advertisement and e-mails.

Sunshine City Hotels
Staff Wanted (Downtown Location)

Passionate about hospitality? We're hiring for our newly renovated downtown location. Various positions available in guest relations, housekeeping, kitchen, and maintenance. No experience? No problem! We provide training. Enjoy competitive benefits and growth opportunities in a welcoming environment. Apply today by sending an e-mail to emma.thompson@schotels.com or visit www.sunshinecityhotels.com. Start your rewarding career in the hospitality industry with us! Note: should be able to start work by July 1st.

To:	Emma Thompson <emma.thompson@schotels.com>
From:	Holly Smith <h.smith@myemail.com>
Subject:	Job Application
Date:	June 5
Attachment:	🖉 Smith résumé

Dear Ms. Thompson,

I hope this e-mail finds you well. I recently came across the job ad for positions at your downtown hotel and I am excited to express my interest. While I may lack professional experience in the hospitality industry, I feel I can contribute greatly in the area of guest relations. I have plenty of experience in an office environment and dealing with clients' needs and requests. While sometimes challenging, I really enjoyed these human connections. I am confident that with the right training, I can quickly adapt and thrive as a full-time employee in a hotel environment.

I look forward to hearing from you.

Sincerely,

Holly Smith

Dear Holly,

It was great to finally meet you last week. I haven't met many people with the same love of skiing that I have. Perhaps I'll see you on the slopes one day.

Thank you for considering our offer of employment at our downtown location and we acknowledge and respect your decision. We really need staff to be able to work from next week, but understand that this did not fit your schedule. There almost certainly will be more positions available in the fall. If you are still keen, please feel free to e-mail me directly to let me know.

We appreciate your interest in our company and wish you the best in your future endeavors.

Sincerely,

Emma Thompson

13. What does the advertisement indicate about Sunshine City Hotel?
   (A) It is hiring one type of position.
   (B) It has more than one location.
   (C) It will open a new location on July 1.
   (D) It is a venue for training conferences.

14. According to the first e-mail, what is true about Ms. Smith?
   (A) She has experience working in a hotel.
   (B) She is interested in a housekeeping position.
   (C) She would like to work part-time.
   (D) She worked with customers in a previous job.

15. In the second e-mail, what can be inferred about Ms. Thompson?
   (A) She had an interview with Ms. Smith.
   (B) She would like to take Ms. Smith skiing.
   (C) She will change the start date for Ms. Smith.
   (D) She will contact Ms. Smith about other future positions.

16. What is most likely true about Ms. Smith?
   (A) She will have a follow-up interview.
   (B) She was asked to work at a different location.
   (C) She was unable to start her job by July 1.
   (D) She was asked to submit more documents.

17. In the second e-mail, the word "keen" in paragraph 2, line 4, is closest in meaning to
   (A) concerned
   (B) interested
   (C) distracted
   (D) indifferent

▶ Incomplete Sentences as REVIEW TEST

Part 5 Select the best choice to complete the sentence.

18. Our HR department is ------- reviewing applications for the open position.
   (A) differently
   (B) currently
   (C) confidently
   (D) directly

19. Candidates who have the proper ------- will be invited for a second-round interview.
   (A) qualify
   (B) qualifications
   (C) qualified
   (D) to qualify

20. She is considering applying ------- the management position.
   (A) for
   (B) by
   (C) to
   (D) in

21. He is an ------- job seeker with a background in finance.
(A) enthusiast
(B) enthusiasm
(C) enthusiastically
(D) enthusiastic

22. Through various recognition programs, we show appreciation for our employees' -------.
(A) inquiries
(B) contributions
(C) applications
(D) certification

23. We are looking for ------- sales professionals who can drive business growth.
(A) experienced
(B) experiences
(C) experiential
(D) experiencing

24. The online application system allows you to attach ------- submit your résumé directly.
(A) neither
(B) but
(C) and
(D) or

TOEIC® L&Rでは、旅行に関する問題がよく出題されます。ホテルなど宿泊先とのメールのやりとり、顧客満足度調査 (customer satisfaction survey) の記入依頼などいくつか頻出する出題パターンがありますので、それらの表現に予め慣れておくとよいでしょう。

≫ TOEIC® L&R頻出ボキャブラリーチェック

▶旅のアドバイス 🔊 Audio ② 23

1. It is crucial to find a _____ _____ in a _____ location to meet your travel needs.　旅のニーズに合わせて便利な場所にあるふさわしい施設を探すことが肝心です。

2. When planning our trip, we should _____ our _____ to fit our budget.
旅行の計画を立てるときは、予算に合う宿泊施設をカスタマイズしましょう。

3. Simplify your trip to _____ by using shuttle services to avoid _____ _____.　交通渋滞を避けるためにシャトルサービスを利用して名所巡りを楽にしましょう。

4. _____ you go to the beach _____ mountains, pack essentials like sunscreen and hiking gear.
海でも山でも、日焼け止めやハイキンググッズなどの必需品を持参しましょう。

▶航空会社とのやりとり

5. The mobile _____ pass will be sent to your _____ e-mail address.
モバイル搭乗券は、ご登録のEメールアドレスに送信されます。

6. Keep your _____ _____ receipts safe until you've successfully collected your _____.
荷物の受け取りが無事完了するまで、手荷物受取証は大切に保管してください。

7. _____ us _____ the app to provide feedback to our airline company.
アプリを通じて当航空会社へのご意見をお寄せください。

▶旅の途中

8. _____ reaching the tour site, _____ at the _____ meeting point.
見学場所に到着次第、指定の集合場所にお集まりください。

9. _____ the high _____, we had a fantastic and impressive desert _____.
暑い気温にもかかわらず、幻想的で印象的な砂漠ツアーとなりました。

10. The hotel's _____ dining is _____ renovations and is temporarily _____ _____ _____.
ホテル館内のダイニングは改装中のため、一時的に営業を停止しています。

≫ **Photographs** 🔊 Audio ② 24-25

Part 1 Please listen to four statements about a photograph. When you hear the statements, you must select one statement from (A), (B), (C), or (D) that best describes the photograph.

1. Ⓐ Ⓑ Ⓒ Ⓓ

2. Ⓐ Ⓑ Ⓒ Ⓓ

≫ **Question-Response** 🔊 Audio ② 26-27

Part 2 Please listen to a question or statement and three responses spoken in English. Then, choose the best response to the question or statement from (A), (B), or (C).

3. Ⓐ Ⓑ Ⓒ
4. Ⓐ Ⓑ Ⓒ
5. Ⓐ Ⓑ Ⓒ
6. Ⓐ Ⓑ Ⓒ

≫ Short Conversations 🔊 Audio ② 28-30

Part 3 Please listen to a short conversation between two or more people. You must listen carefully to understand what the speakers say. You are to choose the best answer to each question.

7. In which department does the woman work?
   (A) Sales
   (B) Production
   (C) Accounting
   (D) Personnel

8. How long will the woman stay in Atlanta?
   (A) Two days
   (B) Three or four days
   (C) A week
   (D) A couple of weeks

9. What does the man suggest the woman do?
   (A) To extend her stay
   (B) To visit a specific facility
   (C) To refrain from consuming soft drinks
   (D) To enjoy a musical show

≫ Short Talks 🔊 Audio ② 31-33

Part 4 Please listen to a short talk. You must listen carefully to understand and remember what is said. You are to choose the best answer to each question.

10. What is the purpose of this advertisement?
    (A) To promote their planning services
    (B) To place an ad in a travel magazine
    (C) To find the best travel destination
    (D) To share unforgettable adventures with their customers

11. How can the experienced agents assist customers?
    (A) Finding five-star hotels in any countries
    (B) Creating custom itineraries tailored to their preferences
    (C) Providing assistance before the departure
    (D) Offering the cheapest optional tour

12. How can customers reach out for assistance?
    (A) Through e-mail or social media platforms
    (B) By visiting the office in person
    (C) By sending a letter by mail
    (D) By making a phone call

Unit

11

旅行③

>> Reading Comprehension

Part 7 Choose the best answer, (A), (B), (C), or (D), to each question.

Questions 13-14 refer to the following information.

Dear Valued Passengers,

Midtown Airport provides a hassle-free baggage claim process to ensure a seamless travel experience for its passengers. Upon arrival, passengers can proceed to the designated baggage claim area, conveniently located near the arrival gates. The area is equipped with conveyor belts that transport luggage from the aircraft to the claim area.

13. Where is the baggage claim area located?
    (A) Near the arrival gates
    (B) Near the departure gates
    (C) Near the customs area
    (D) Near the security checkpoint

14. What does Midtown Airport provide for passengers?
    (A) A separate check-in area
    (B) Complimentary snacks
    (C) Dedicated conveyor belts
    (D) VIP lounge access

Questions 15-17 refer to the following survey.

Please rate each item on a scale of 1 (poor) to 5 (excellent) and provide any additional comments or suggestions. Your feedback is valuable to us in improving our services.

1.	Check-in Process: Was the check-in process efficient and friendly?	(5)
2.	Room Cleanliness: Was the room clean and well-maintained?	(5)
3.	Comfort: Was the bed comfortable and the room temperature suitable?	(2)

4.	Amenities: Were the amenities provided in the room satisfactory?	(5)
5.	Staff Interaction: Were the hotel staff friendly, helpful, and responsive to your needs?	(4)
6.	Room Service/Food: How was the quality and timeliness of room service or on-site dining?	N/A
7.	Facilities: Did the hotel have adequate facilities such as a gym, pool, or spa?	(5)
8.	Noise Level: Was the hotel quiet and conducive to a good night's sleep?	(3)
9.	Location: Was the hotel conveniently located for your needs?	(5)
10.	Overall Experience: Based on your stay, would you recommend this hotel to others?	(4)

Comments and suggestions:

Overall, my hotel stay was satisfactory. The check-in process was efficient, and the room cleanliness was commendable. However, the bed was not as comfortable as expected, affecting my sleep quality. Despite this, the convenient location, which was the biggest advantage, and the adequate facilities made my stay manageable. I would recommend the hotel on the condition that they improve the bed.

15. What is suggested from the checklist?
    (A) The hotel staff were not friendly and responsive.
    (B) The guest didn't use any room service.
    (C) The location of the hotel was not satisfactory.
    (D) The bed was as comfortable as expected.

16. In the comments and suggestions, the word "commendable" in paragraph 1, line 2, is closest in meaning to
    (A) outstanding   (C) disappointing
    (B) mediocre   (D) inefficient

17. What was the main issue the guest had with the hotel stay?
    (A) Room location   (C) Room comfort
    (B) Room cleanliness   (D) Room service quality

▶ Incomplete Sentences as REVIEW TEST

Select the best choice to complete the sentence.

18. The online booking system allows you to easily search for suitable and ------- flight options.
(A) convention
(B) conveniently
(C) convenient
(D) convenience

19. ------- you choose to travel by plane or train, make sure to book your tickets in advance.
(A) So
(B) Whether
(C) Although
(D) Either

20. Some people share their travel experiences ------- their social media platforms.
(A) through
(B) within
(C) over
(D) while

21. Upon ------- in at the airport, we proceeded to the security checkpoint.
(A) check
(B) checked
(C) to check
(D) checking

22. There was a ------- section in the museum where photography was not allowed.
(A) designated
(B) tailored
(C) appointed
(D) reserved

23. ------- the traffic congestion, we arrived at the hotel later than expected.
(A) Despite
(B) Because of
(C) Therefore
(D) Since

24. The hiking trail was ------- repairs, requiring us to take an alternative route.
(A) completing
(B) conducting
(C) undergoing
(D) contacting

天気・環境 ————————————————

TOEIC® L&Rでは、天気・環境に関する問題がほぼ毎々出題されます。悪天候に伴う交通機関の混乱、社内イベントなどのスケジュールの変更、環境問題への取り組みなどいくつか頻出する出題パターンがありますので、それらの表現に予め慣れておくとよいでしょう。

≫ TOEIC® L&R頻出ボキャブラリーチェック

▶気象・天候・農業に関する表現 🔊 Audio ②34

1. The _____ always checks the _____ _____.
   造園業者は常に天気予報をチェックしています。

2. After the storm, I had to _____ the damaged _____ and clean the patio by _____.
   嵐の後、私は傷んだ葉を刈り取り、テラスを掃き掃除しなくてはなりませんでした。

3. _____ efficient irrigation techniques is _____.
   効率的な灌漑技術の導入は極めて重要です。

4. _____ _____ _____ rainfall has _____ worsened the _____ conditions.
   雨不足が干ばつ状態をかなり悪化させています。

5. Drought-resistant _____ play a _____ role.
   干ばつに強い作物は重要な役割を果たしています。

▶環境問題への対応に関する表現

6. Make sure to use the _____ bins to _____ of recyclable materials properly.
   リサイクル可能な資材を廃棄するには必ず指定された容器を使用してください。

7. Our company is taking _____ _____ to reduce its _____ impact.
   当社は環境への影響を軽減するための有意な対策を講じています。

8. It is _____ to _____ the global _____ and find effective solutions.
   世界的な問題に取り組み、効果的な解決策を見つけることが不可欠です。

9. The company is committed to using renewable _____ _____ _____.
   その会社は再生可能な原材料の使用に取り組んでいます。

10. Investing in _____ energy is a key step towards a _____ future.
    再生可能エネルギーへの投資は、持続可能な未来に向けた重要な一歩です。

Listening Parts

>> Photographs 🔊 Audio ② 35-36

Part 1   Please listen to four statements about a photograph. When you hear the statements, you must select one statement from (A), (B), (C), or (D) that best describes the photograph.

1. Ⓐ Ⓑ Ⓒ Ⓓ

2. Ⓐ Ⓑ Ⓒ Ⓓ

>> Question-Response 🔊 Audio ② 37-38

Part 2   Please listen to a question or statement and three responses spoken in English. Then, choose the best response to the question or statement from (A), (B), or (C).

3. Ⓐ Ⓑ Ⓒ
4. Ⓐ Ⓑ Ⓒ
5. Ⓐ Ⓑ Ⓒ
6. Ⓐ Ⓑ Ⓒ

>> Short Conversations 🔊 Audio ② 39-41

Part 3 Please listen to a short conversation between two or more people. You must listen carefully to understand what the speakers say. You are to choose the best answer to each question.

Weather Forecast

| Monday | Tuesday | Wednesday | Thursday | Friday |

7. Who most likely is the woman?
   (A) A weather forecaster
   (B) A BBQ restaurant manager
   (C) A company event organizer
   (D) A park office employee

8. Look at the graphic. What day is the event originally planned for?
   (A) Tuesday
   (B) Wednesday
   (C) Thursday
   (D) Friday

9. What will the man do next?
   (A) Make a phone call
   (B) Attend a meeting
   (C) Talk to a manager
   (D) Visit the woman again

>> Short Talks 🔊 Audio ② 42-44

Part 4 Please listen to a short talk. You must listen carefully to understand and remember what is said. You are to choose the best answer to each question.

DEPARTURES				
10:50	NEW YORK	AC 103	BOARDING	Gate 12
10:55	TORONTO	KA 198	ON TIME	Gate 13
11:20	SYDNEY	FM 324	DELAYED	Gate 15
11:30	SINGAPORE	CI5668	ON TIME	Gate 18

10. Why are some flights being delayed?
    (A) They are waiting for repairs to finish.
    (B) They are currently experiencing bad weather.
    (C) Bad weather has damaged the airplanes.
    (D) Bad weather has affected the entire schedule.

11. Look at the graphic. Which flight will likely experience a change in departure information?
(A) New York
(B) Toronto
(C) Sydney
(D) Singapore

12. According to the speaker, what is the most efficient way to get the latest flight information?
(A) Check the airport app
(B) Await an announcement
(C) Approach a nearby staff member
(D) Visit the airport website

▶ Reading Parts

≫ Text Comprehension

Part 6 Select the best choice to complete the text.

Questions 13-16 refer to the following article.

Conference on Drought Issues Seeks Sustainable Solutions

(29 September, Adelaide) The Conference on Preventing Drought ------- in
__13.__
Adelaide on 28 September, bringing together experts and stakeholders to

------- the escalating global drought problem. -------. Experts emphasised
__14.__   __15.__
the significance of enhanced drought-tolerant crops and advanced irrigation

technologies. Craig Simon, a representative of the conference organiser,

acknowledged the challenge of solving this global issue within individual

regions but expressed hope in ------- regional leadership and cooperation
                               __16.__
to promote sustainable measures. With a shared commitment, they aim to

tackle the issue collaboratively and drive impactful change.

---

13. (A) was taken place
    (B) took place
    (C) will take place
    (D) had taken place

14. (A) address
    (B) bring
    (C) make
    (D) prepare

15. (A) The implementation of irrigation systems enables them to make informed decisions.
    (B) Such a technique involves applying water directly to the root zone of plants.
    (C) As this issue grows increasingly severe, participants focused on sustainable solutions.
    (D) They provide farmers with more reliable and sustainable options.

16. (A) strengthless
    (B) strong
    (C) strength
    (D) strengthening

>> Reading Comprehension

Part 7 Choose the best answer, (A), (B), (C), or (D), to each question.

Questions 17-19 refer to the following article.

Small talk is an essential part of establishing connections and fostering relationships in the business world. While conversations may vary, one topic that often emerges as a common icebreaker is the weather. Despite its seemingly trivial nature, discussing the weather can serve as a gateway to deeper conversations and provide a shared experience between individuals.

Weather-related small talk in business settings can serve multiple purposes. It helps break the initial tension, creates a friendly atmosphere, and offers a neutral topic that transcends professional boundaries. Furthermore, discussing weather conditions can be relevant in various industries, such as agriculture, tourism, or construction, where weather patterns significantly impact operations and decision-making.

Engaging in weather-related small talk demonstrates social skills and the ability to connect on a human level. By showing genuine interest and acknowledging the impact of weather on daily life or business operations, professionals can establish rapport, leading to more meaningful conversations and potential opportunities for collaboration.

17. What is the purpose of the article?
   (A) To report on the importance of weather forecasts on business
   (B) To show how to outline business ideas during small talk
   (C) To inform on the role of weather in business small talk
   (D) To discuss multiple relationships among industries

18. Why is weather-related small talk important in business?
   (A) It establishes rapport.
   (B) It showcases technical knowledge.
   (C) It promotes competitiveness.
   (D) It guarantees success.

19. In the article, the word "transcends" in paragraph 2, line 3, is closest in meaning to
   (A) stops over   (C) goes beyond
   (B) refrains from   (D) makes sure

▶ Incomplete Sentences as REVIEW TEST

Part 5 Select the best choice to complete the sentence.

20. The city has ------- bike lanes for cyclists to ensure their safety.
   (A) to be designated
   (B) designating
   (C) designates
   (D) designated

21. She carefully ------- of the old documents by shredding them.
   (A) renovated
   (B) eliminated
   (C) disposed
   (D) removed

22. The weather station provides ------- data for meteorologists to predict weather patterns.
   (A) essence
   (B) essentials
   (C) essential
   (D) essentially

23. Local communities are organizing clean-up campaigns to ------- the issue of littering.
(A) address
(B) disagree
(C) take
(D) launch

24. The project team created a detailed plan to deal with the global issues and ------- it.
(A) implements
(B) implemented
(C) implementation
(D) implementing

25. Renewable energy -------, such as solar power, are gaining popularity due to their environmental benefits.
(A) causes
(B) sources
(C) roots
(D) statistics

26. Climate change ------- impacts the Earth's ecosystems and weather patterns.
(A) signified
(B) significant
(C) significance
(D) significantly

娯楽・スポーツ ────────────

TOEIC® L&Rでは、リスニングでもリーディングでも娯楽やスポーツに関する問題がしばしば出題されます。ピクニック、健康維持のための運動、スポーツ観戦、音楽、美術、演劇などの芸術鑑賞など表現について慣れておくとよいでしょう。

>> **TOEIC® L&R頻出ボキャブラリーチェック**

▶ チケット販売について 🔊 Audio ② 45

1. Please make sure to stand _____ _____ _____ and wait for your turn.
   必ず一列にお並びいただき、順番をお待ちください。

2. The _____ offer for early birds allows them to _____ tickets before they _____ _____ _____ to everyone else.
   早期購入者の限定特典は、一般販売より先にチケットを確保することができます。

▶ **美術館やイベントなどでの表現**

3. The stadium was _____ _____ _____ _____.
   スタジアムは熱狂的な観客で埋め尽くされていました。

4. The fans _____ _____ _____ witness a close game that went into extra innings.　ファンは延長戦にもつれ込む接戦を目の当たりにして大興奮でした。

5. The _____ _____ _____ _____ near the main entrance.
   売店は正面入り口の近くにあります。

6. The gallery curator will carefully _____ the _____ for the upcoming _____.　その画廊の学芸員は次の展覧会のための彫刻作品を慎重に決定する予定です。

7. The museum's collection of artifacts _____ _____ a connection to the past and cultural _____.
   博物館の工芸品コレクションは、過去と文化遺産のつながりを育む手助けになっています。

8. With the _____ app, visitors can receive audio instructions _____ _____ the museum _____.
   専用アプリで、来館者は博物館の展示物を見学しながら音声による説明を受けることができます。

9. We _____ _____ hike _____ _____ _____ of Mt. Moon _____ _____ _____.　私たちは月山の景色の良い登山道を一日中歩くことに賛成です。

10. As a _____ of appreciation, each participant received a packet of _____ flower seeds.
    感謝の印として、各参加者が珍しい花の種の詰め合わせを受け取りました。

Listening Parts

>> Photographs 🔊 Audio ② 46-47

Part 1 Please listen to four statements about a photograph. When you hear the statements, you must select one statement from (A), (B), (C), or (D) that best describes the photograph.

1. Ⓐ Ⓑ Ⓒ Ⓓ

2. Ⓐ Ⓑ Ⓒ Ⓓ

>> Question-Response 🔊 Audio ② 48-49

Part 2 Please listen to a question or statement and three responses spoken in English. Then, choose the best response to the question or statement from (A), (B), or (C).

3. Ⓐ Ⓑ Ⓒ
4. Ⓐ Ⓑ Ⓒ
5. Ⓐ Ⓑ Ⓒ
6. Ⓐ Ⓑ Ⓒ

Part 3   Please listen to a short conversation between two or more people. You must listen carefully to understand what the speakers say. You are to choose the best answer to each question.

JULY	
Saturday	1
Sunday	2
Monday	3
Tuesday	4

7. What activity does the man want to do on Saturday?
   (A) Hiking
   (B) Visiting an art gallery
   (C) Watching a movie
   (D) Playing sports

8. What is the exhibition about at the art gallery?
   (A) Classic art
   (B) Modern art
   (C) Nature photography
   (D) Sculptures

9. Look at the graphic. When do the speakers plan to visit the art gallery?
   (A) Saturday
   (B) Sunday
   (C) Monday
   (D) Tuesday

>> Short Talks 🔊 Audio ② 53-55

Part 4 Please listen to a short talk. You must listen carefully to understand and remember what is said. You are to choose the best answer to each question.

Back Entrance

West Entrance   East Entrance

Main Entrance

10. Where does the announcement most likely take place?
    (A) At a musical theater
    (B) At a ballpark
    (C) At a grocery store
    (D) At a convention center

11. When can people start making baseball tickets reservations?
    (A) Next month
    (B) Soon after the announcement
    (C) Only on match days
    (D) Six months in advance

12. Look at the graphic. Where should people go to get their tickets in person?
    (A) West Entrance
    (B) Main Entrance
    (C) East Entrance
    (D) Back Entrance

» Reading Comprehension

Part 7 Choose the best answer, (A), (B), (C), or (D), to each question.

Questions 13-15 refer to the following web page.

https://www.frespringathleticclub.com/partner

Inviting Partnerships with Frespring Athletic Club
Building the Future Together for the Community

Frespring Athletic Club is seeking new sponsorship partners to support the development of the local sports culture and nurture young talents. We extend this unique sponsorship opportunity to companies and organizations. —[1]—

Founded in 1967, Frespring Athletic Club stands as a leading soccer club representing our region, backed by passionate supporters and promising young players.

By participating in our sponsorship program, you can benefit from:

Strong Brand Exposure: Showcase your company's logo on our official jerseys and utilize advertising space at match venues to reach a wide audience and enhance brand visibility. —[2]—

Strengthening Community Communication: Foster closer ties with the local community through collaboration in club events and social initiatives, building trust with the people in the region.

Exclusive Company Events and Rewards Program: Offer your employees and partners special privileges, including match invitations and discounted tickets, as a token of appreciation.

Supporting Young Sports Talent: Contribute to the development of young soccer athletes and nurture sports talent within the community.

If you are interested in becoming a sponsorship partner or have any inquiries, please don't hesitate to send an email to *info@frespringathleticclub.com*. —[3]—

Frespring Athletic Club is eagerly looking forward to your support. —[4]—
Let's build an incredible partnership with the soccer club that represents the
community and shapes a bright future together!

13. What is the purpose of the web page?
    (A) To request feedback of a unique service
    (B) To encourage participation in a regional event
    (C) To look for sponsorship partners
    (D) To announce a new product

14. What is NOT mentioned as a benefit of the sponsorship program?
    (A) Game invitations and discounted tickets
    (B) Participation in networking events
    (C) Access to tax benefits
    (D) Company exposure on team uniforms

15. In which of the positions marked [1], [2], [3], and [4] does the following
sentence best belong?
    "They should share our vision of contributing to the growth and success
of the community."
    (A) [1]
    (B) [2]
    (C) [3]
    (D) [4]

Questions 16-17 refer to the following text-message chain.

> **James McDonald (10:55 A.M.)**
> Hi Sally, any chance that we can reschedule the 11:15 CompuTime meeting until after lunch? This 10:00 meeting is running long.

> **Sally Yamada (10:57 A.M.)**
> No can do. They have arrived early and are waiting in the conference room as we speak.

> **James McDonald (10:59 A.M.)**
> In that case, you may have to start without me. Is that okay?

> **Sally Yamada (11:01 A.M.)**
> Got it. The presentation is on my computer anyway. Just try not to be too late since you were supposed to explain all the numbers, and CompuTime will be more interested in that.

16. Why does Mr. McDonald contact Ms. Yamada?
(A) To schedule a conference
(B) To make plans for lunch
(C) To ask about CompuTime numbers
(D) To change a meeting time

17. At 11:01 A.M., what does Ms. Yamada mean when she writes, "Got it."?
(A) She has the computer file for the meeting.
(B) She received Mr. McDonald's message.
(C) She accepts the idea of beginning the meeting alone.
(D) She agreed to speak about the numbers.

Part 5 Select the best choice to complete the sentence.

18. Maintain a relaxed posture ------- breathing deeply during the yoga practice.
    (A) until   (C) within
    (B) while   (D) instead

19. The loyal supporters agreed ------- a block of seats to cheer on their favorite team.
    (A) to reserve   (C) reserving
    (B) reserve   (D) reservation

20. The outdoor concert featured a lineup of talented musicians ------- the night.
    (A) throughout   (C) because of
    (B) therefore   (D) although

21. Cycling is a great way to help you ------- the outdoors.
    (A) explores   (C) explore
    (B) exploration   (D) explored

22. Through the event's official website, exclusive backstage tour tickets are ------- sale.
    (A) to   (C) in
    (B) at   (D) on

23. The rugby coach praised the team for their ------- and aggressive gameplay.
    (A) excitement   (C) exciting
    (B) excite   (D) excited

24. The event was so popular that people lined up in a ------- for hours to get their tickets.
    (A) rank   (C) row
    (B) string   (D) chain

Unit

13

娯楽・スポーツ

会議

TOEIC® L&Rでは、リスニングでもリーディングでも会議に関する問題がほぼ毎回出題されます。議事録の作成、スケジュールの変更、出欠の確認、議案などの表現について慣れておくとよいでしょう。

≫ TOEIC® L&R頻出ボキャブラリーチェック

▶会議でよく使われる表現 🔊 Audio ② 56

1. I'd like to express my ＿＿＿＿ ＿＿＿＿ everyone's attendance in today's meeting.　本日のミーティングにご出席いただいた皆様に感謝申し上げます。

2. ＿＿＿＿ you have an ＿＿＿＿ or need clarification, ＿＿＿＿ ＿＿＿＿ ＿＿＿＿ raise your hand and speak up.
ご質問、ご不明な点などございましたら、遠慮なく手を挙げて発言してください。

▶意見や状況を述べる表現

3. We should ＿＿＿＿ ＿＿＿＿ ＿＿＿＿ to gather valuable insights.
貴重な意見を収集するためにアンケートを実施した方が良いと思います。

4. We ＿＿＿＿ ＿＿＿＿ ＿＿＿＿ to reach our sales ＿＿＿＿ for this quarter.
今期の販売ノルマを順調に達成しそうです。

5. I ＿＿＿＿ exploring ＿＿＿＿ target markets to expand our customer base.
顧客基盤を拡大するために、潜在的なターゲット市場を開拓することを提案します。

6. If we don't ＿＿＿＿ the customer ＿＿＿＿ ＿＿＿＿, they could harm our ＿＿＿＿.
顧客からの苦情に迅速に対処しなければ、評判を落とすことになりかねません。

7. Work efficiency can be improved ＿＿＿＿ ＿＿＿＿ the ＿＿＿＿ tools in the office.
オフィスに最先端ツールを導入すれば、作業効率が改善されます。

8. We are ＿＿＿＿ a year-end ＿＿＿＿ to ＿＿＿＿ the ＿＿＿＿ of our employees.
当社は社員の功績を称えるため、年末に祝賀会を開催しています。

▶その他

9. Effective communication can ＿＿＿＿ misunderstandings that can later ＿＿＿＿ ＿＿＿＿ as ＿＿＿＿.
効果的なコミュニケーションは、後に混乱した考えとして積み重なる誤解を防ぐことができます。

10. Please remember that only ＿＿＿＿ attendees are allowed to participate in this meeting.　この会議に参加できるのは、許可された出席者のみであることをご留意ください。

11. The software will only be available for ＿＿＿＿ use ＿＿＿＿ a permanent license is purchased.
永続的なライセンスを購入しない限り、そのソフトウェアは一時的にしか利用できません。

▶ Listening Parts

≫ Photographs 🔊 Audio ② 57-58

Part 1 Please listen to four statements about a photograph. When you hear the statements, you must select one statement from (A), (B), (C), or (D) that best describes the photograph.

1. Ⓐ Ⓑ Ⓒ Ⓓ

2. Ⓐ Ⓑ Ⓒ Ⓓ

≫ Question-Response 🔊 Audio ② 59-60

Part 2 Please listen to a question or statement and three responses spoken in English. Then, choose the best response to the question or statement from (A), (B), or (C).

3. Ⓐ Ⓑ Ⓒ
4. Ⓐ Ⓑ Ⓒ
5. Ⓐ Ⓑ Ⓒ
6. Ⓐ Ⓑ Ⓒ

≫ Short Conversations 🔊 Audio ② 61-63

Part 3 Please listen to a short conversation between two or more people. You must listen carefully to understand what the speakers say. You are to choose the best answer to each question.

Questions 7-9 are on the next page.

7. Where most likely are the speakers?
(A) At a seminar
(B) At a hotel
(C) At an office
(D) At an airport

8. What does the woman imply when she says, "I couldn't make it."?
(A) She made a project proposal.
(B) She presented four potential ideas.
(C) She was absent at the meeting.
(D) She asked several questions about the next venture.

9. What will the speakers do next?
(A) Organize their ideas
(B) Reschedule a meeting
(C) Prepare a new project
(D) Decide a potential leader

» Short Talks 🔊 Audio ② 64-66

Part 4 Please listen to a short talk. You must listen carefully to understand and remember what is said. You are to choose the best answer to each question.

Global Board Meeting	
Date	Place
January 7th	New York
April 6th	London
July 14th	Tokyo
October 4th	Paris

10. Look at the graphic. Where will the next global board meeting be held?
(A) New York
(B) London
(C) Tokyo
(D) Paris

11. Who most likely is the speaker?
(A) The CEO
(B) A technical assistant
(C) A financial manager
(D) An environmental specialist

12. According to the speaker, what are the listeners expected to do?
(A) To turn this company around for the next quarter
(B) To attend the meeting with data-based insights and ideas
(C) To create an environmentally-friendly product
(D) To reorganize the meeting agenda

Reading Parts

>> Reading Comprehension

Part 7 Choose the best answer, (A), (B), (C), or (D), to each question.

Questions 13-17 refer to the following sign and e-mail.

Attention All Solar Express Employees:

To conserve energy and reduce paper waste, please follow these guidelines when using the office copier:

1. Print double-sided whenever possible
2. Print in grayscale unless color is necessary
3. Use the "Print Preview" function
4. Collect your printouts promptly to prevent unauthorized access
5. Always remember, recycle when possible

Thank you for your cooperation in our sustainability efforts.

- Office Management

To: All Employees
From: Ken Suzuki <kensuzuki@solarexpresscompany.com>
Subject: Copier Guidelines
Date: April 3

Hi everyone,

I just wanted to remind everyone about the new guidelines for using the office printer. It's important that we all do our part to conserve energy and reduce paper waste.

I have had a lot of inquiries as to how to recycle. There was no container to collect used paper, so that will be taken care of. Thank you for pointing this out.

There have also been a couple of questions about the third guideline listed. By doing this each time, we can avoid having to print again, which will help cut down on waste.

Lastly, please don't forget to pick up your printouts as soon as they're done printing. It's not only for security reasons but also helps to keep the printer area uncluttered which is good for everyone.

Let's work together to make our office more sustainable!

Best regards,
Ken Suzuki
Office Manager, Solar Express

13. What is the purpose of the sign on the printer?
(A) To provide instructions for using the printer
(B) To announce a maintenance schedule
(C) To inform about a printer malfunction
(D) To advertise a new printer model

14. According to the sign, when should you use color printing?
(A) Only when absolutely necessary
(B) For all print jobs
(C) Only when printing photos
(D) When printing on both sides

15. According to the e-mail, what also helps to reduce paper waste?
(A) Printing double-sided
(B) Using the print preview function
(C) Sending electronic documents
(D) Picking up the printed materials immediately

16. What did Mr. Suzuki get many questions about?
(A) Use of greyscale   (C) Recycling details
(B) Unauthorized access   (D) Print use times

17. In the e-mail, the word "uncluttered" in paragraph 4, line 3, is closest in meaning to
(A) tidy   (C) messy
(B) spacious   (D) workable

▶Incomplete Sentences as REVIEW TEST

Part 5 Select the best choice to complete the sentence.

18. Adjust the display settings according to the room's lighting conditions ------- using the projector.
(A) when
(B) how
(C) despite
(D) such as

19. The minutes of the meeting were shared ------- to keep all stakeholders informed.
(A) prompt
(B) promptly
(C) prompting
(D) promptness

20. The meeting won't be productive ------- everyone comes prepared with their progress updates.
(A) because
(B) however
(C) unless
(D) though

21. The research team proposed an innovative methodology ------- more accurate data analysis.
(A) to achieve
(B) achieve
(C) achievement
(D) achievable

22. Our company regularly ------- training sessions to enhance employee skills.
(A) omits
(B) conducts
(C) prevents
(D) inquiries

23. Today's meeting is not only for discussing agendas but ------- for building consensus among team members.
(A) yet
(B) usually
(C) always
(D) also

24. The manager began the meeting by expressing gratitude ------- everyone's attendance and contributions.
(A) at
(B) for
(C) to
(D) on

Listening Parts

» Photographs

Part 1 Please listen to four statements about a photograph. When you hear the statements, you must select one statement from (A), (B), (C), or (D) that best describes the photograph.

1. Ⓐ Ⓑ Ⓒ Ⓓ

2. Ⓐ Ⓑ Ⓒ Ⓓ

» Question-Response

Part 2 Please listen to a question or statement and three responses spoken in English. Then, choose the best response to the question or statement from (A), (B), or (C).

3. Ⓐ Ⓑ Ⓒ
4. Ⓐ Ⓑ Ⓒ
5. Ⓐ Ⓑ Ⓒ
6. Ⓐ Ⓑ Ⓒ

≫ Short Conversations

Part 3 Please listen to a short conversation between two or more people. You must listen carefully to understand what the speakers say. You are to choose the best answer to each question.

7. What is the minimum age the woman mentions as the eligibility for early retirement?
   (A) 50 years old
   (B) 55 years old
   (C) 60 years old
   (D) 65 years old

8. What benefits does the early retirement system offer?
   (A) Stock options
   (B) Tuition reimbursement
   (C) Pension top-ups and health coverage
   (D) Company car allowance

9. What will the man do next?
   (A) Share his plans with the woman
   (B) Check his qualification for the early retirement
   (C) Leave the company with a great incentive
   (D) Contact HR to get more information

≫ Short Talks

Part 4 Please listen to a short talk. You must listen carefully to understand and remember what is said. You are to choose the best answer to each question.

10. What is the topic of today's broadcast?
    (A) The strength of individual skills
    (B) The reasons for supporting a sports team
    (C) An advertisement of a sports event
    (D) An apology for a schedule change

11. What are the listeners encouraged to do?
    (A) To meet a fan club owner
    (B) To describe a favorite team
    (C) To become a fan club member
    (D) To donate money to a sports team

12. What can the listeners do on the website?
    (A) Ask players questions
    (B) Watch live games
    (C) View information about sports teams
    (D) Buy their favorite team's goods

>> Text Comprehension

Part 6 Select the best choice to complete the text.

Questions 13-16 refer to the following article.

TechCaree Launches Technician Careers Campaign

TechCaree, a nonprofit company, has launched its annual campaign. The campaign is showcased on the TechCaree website and social media, and features a diverse group of individuals sharing their stories of ------- technician careers. -------.
  13.   14.
To encourage people with interests ------- skilled technician careers,
                                     15.
the TechCaree website includes a weekly feature that showcases persons in skilled technician jobs, ------- share their stories in short
                                              16.
video interviews.

---

13. (A) adjustable
    (B) prospective
    (C) successful
    (D) affordable

14. (A) Participants earn points and prizes by accessing training.
    (B) Launching an online business can seem difficult.
    (C) The most efficient e-commerce platforms keep it simple.
    (D) This includes technicians' testimonials across various industry sectors.

15. (A) at   (C) in
    (B) of   (D) about

16. (A) what   (C) which
    (B) who   (D) how

>> Reading Comprehension

Part 7 Choose the best answer, (A), (B), (C), or (D), to each question.

Questions 17-21 refer to the following e-mails.

To: David Lee <davidlee@quicksavemagazine.com>
From: Mari Kondo <marikondo@carcircus.com>
Subject: Proposal for Collaborative Marketing Campaign
Date: July 17
Attachment: 📎 Our proposal

Dear David Lee,

I hope this email finds you well. I enjoyed our discussion at the sales conference last week. I'm following up on the idea that we talked about concerning collaborating on future projects.

We have a few concepts in mind so I've attached a detailed proposal outlining some more information and key points of our suggested collaboration.

When you have time, check out the proposal and let me know your thoughts. We're open to any suggestions or modifications you might have. If this collaboration interests you, we can arrange a meeting at your convenience to talk more about the details. If possible, a meeting near the end of the month, or the beginning of next month would be ideal. A meeting after that will be a little trickier to manage.

Looking forward to your feedback.

Best regards,

Mari Kondo
Marketing Assistant
Car Circus

To: Mari Kondo <marikondo@carcircus.com>
From: David Lee <davidlee@quicksavemagazine.com>
Subject: Re: Proposal for Collaborative Marketing Campaign
Date: July 20

Dear Mari Kondo,

Thank you for reaching out and for your interest in a potential collaboration. I've had the chance to review the attached proposal and discuss it with my team. Overall, we find the idea alluring and believe there could be some value in a future project.

I have a few questions and clarifications regarding the proposed campaign:
- What would be the specific timeline for this campaign?
- In the proposal, it mentions a budget allocation for the campaign. Could you provide more details about how this budget would be utilized?
- Have you identified the target audience for this campaign?
- Are there any legal or contractual considerations we need to be aware of before moving forward?
- Can you provide examples of successful collaborations your company has undertaken in the past?

Once we have a clearer understanding of these things, we can schedule a meeting to go into the finer details and potential next steps. I understand your scheduling difficulties so accommodating your first scheduling suggestion should be no problem.

Thank you again for considering this collaboration. We look forward to your response.

Best regards,

David Lee
Assistant Analyst
Quick Save Magazine

17. What is the purpose of Ms. Kondo's e-mail to Mr. Lee?
    (A) To discuss a recent sales conference
    (B) To propose a marketing collaboration
    (C) To inquire about a job opening
    (D) To share a personal update

18. How will Mr. Lee get more detailed information from Ms. Kondo?
    (A) In a telephone call
    (B) In an e-mail attachment
    (C) At a future sales conference
    (D) At a meeting

19. What does Mr. Lee inquire about in relation to legal considerations?
    (A) Whether Ms. Kondo is interested in a job position
    (B) How the proposal aligns with company goals
    (C) Potential target audience demographics
    (D) Any legal or contractual aspects to consider

20. When most likely will they have their meeting?
    (A) At the end of this month
    (B) At the beginning of next month
    (C) In the middle of this month
    (D) In the middle of next month

21. In the second e-mail, the word "alluring" in paragraph 1, line 3, is closest in meaning to
    (A) objectionable
    (B) interesting
    (C) unsuitable
    (D) questionable

Incomplete Sentences as REVIEW TEST

Part 5 Select the best choice to complete the sentence.

22. We will be sending you the ------- sales quote by the end of the week.
    (A) expecting
    (B) to expect
    (C) expect
    (D) expected

23. Our innovative approach has helped us maintain a competitive position ------- the market conditions are challenging.
    (A) instead of
    (B) despite
    (C) due to
    (D) although

24. Many people prefer ------- the holiday in a cozy cabin in the mountains.
    (A) attempting
    (B) spending
    (C) dropping
    (D) visiting

25. The state-of-the-art ------- facility offers a range of amenities to cater to the needs of business tenants.
    (A) commercially
    (B) commercial
    (C) commerce
    (D) commercialize

26. The flexible work policy has ------- employees to choose their preferred work hours.
    (A) applied
    (B) resulted
    (C) completed
    (D) allowed

27. In order to maintain a positive work culture, we need to take care of ------- and prioritize work-life balance.
    (A) us
    (B) we
    (C) ourselves
    (D) our

28. The company's revenue has been increasing ------- due to the successful launch of the innovative product.
    (A) rapidly
    (B) frequently
    (C) generously
    (D) alternatively

Vocabulary List

本書で扱った語彙リストです。テキストだけでなくリスニングのスクリプトに出題の語彙・表現も含まれます。
英語 → 日本語、日本語 → 英語と覚えたら、□に印を入れて予習・復習に役立てましょう。

▶ 各品詞の略称 名=名詞 動=動詞 形=形容詞 副=副詞 前=前置詞 接=接続詞

A

	語彙・表現		品詞 意味	Unit
□	a range of	□	さまざまな〜、〜の範囲の、広範囲の〜	1, 8, 15
□	a variety of	□	様々な〜	5, 8
□	ability	□	名 能力	3, 4, 5, 10, 12
□	absent	□	形 不在の	7, 14
□	absolutely	□	副 絶対に、全く、もちろん	14
□	accept	□	動 受け入れる	2, 6, 13
□	acclaim	□	動 称賛する、高く評価する	1
□	accommodate	□	動 収容する、応える、満たす	3, 6, 8
□	accommodation	□	名 宿泊施設、ホテル	6, 11
□	accomplish	□	動 成し遂げる	2
□	accurate	□	形 正確な	4, 5, 9, 14
□	achieve	□	動 達成する	7, 14, 15
□	achievement	□	名 達成	7, 14, 15
□	acknowledge	□	動 認める、承認する	10, 12
□	activated	□	形 作動している、活動している	8
□	adapt	□	動 適応する	6, 10
□	address an issue	□	問題に対処する	12
□	adjust	□	動 調整する	11, 14, 15
□	adjustable	□	形 調整可能な	8, 15
□	admission	□	名 入場料	1
□	advanced	□	形 上級の、進歩した、先進的な	5, 12, 14
□	advantage	□	名 利点	4, 11, 15
□	advertise	□	動 宣伝する	14
□	afford	□	動 (金銭的、時間的) 余裕がある	6
□	affordable	□	形 お手頃な	3, 6, 8, 15
□	agenda	□	名 議題	2, 14, 15
□	agree to *do*	□	*do* するのに賛成する	13
□	aisle	□	名 通路	6
□	allow	□	動 許す、許可する	1, 2, 6, 10, 11, 13, 14, 15
□	allowance	□	名 手当、許容	15
□	alternative	□	形 代替の、代わりの	2, 11
□	alternatively	□	副 代わりに、あるいは	15
□	although	□	接 にもかかわらず	5, 7, 9, 11, 13, 15
□	analysis	□	名 分析	14, 15
□	annual	□	形 年次の、年1回の	2, 15
□	anticipate	□	動 期待する	4
□	apologize	□	動 謝る、謝罪する	2, 8
□	apology	□	名 謝罪	1, 2, 6, 15
□	appetite	□	名 食欲	3, 5
□	appetizing	□	形 食欲をそそるような、美味しそうな	3
□	appliance	□	名 電化製品	8
□	application	□	名 申込書、応募、申込	10
□	apply	□	動 適用する、申し込む	7, 10
□	apply for	□	〜に申し込む	2, 5, 10
□	appointment	□	名 予約、約束	5, 15
□	appreciate	□	動 感謝する	2, 3, 4, 7, 8, 9, 10
□	appreciation	□	名 感謝	2, 7, 10, 13
□	appreciative	□	形 感謝している	2, 3
□	appropriate	□	形 適切な、きちんとした	1, 5
□	approve	□	動 承認する	2
□	approximately	□	副 およそ	1

	品詞 意味	Unit
☐ aspect	☐ 名 側面、見方	5, 15
☐ assemble	☐ 動 組み立てる	15
☐ assignment	☐ 名 課題、割り当てられた任務	7
☐ assure	☐ 動 保証する、請け合う	8
☐ atmosphere	☐ 名 雰囲気	3, 12, 13
☐ attach	☐ 動 添付する、付ける	10, 15
☐ attachment	☐ 名 添付、添付書類	6, 10, 15
☐ attempt	☐ 動 試す	15
☐ attendee	☐ 名 出席者	2, 4, 14
☐ attract	☐ 動 魅了する	4
☐ attractive	☐ 形 魅力的な	9, 15
☐ audience	☐ 名 観客、聴衆	2, 4, 10, 13, 15
☐ authentic	☐ 形 本格的な	1, 3
☐ availability	☐ 名 可能性、可能	3, 8
☐ available	☐ 形 可能な、入手できる	1, 3, 6, 8, 9, 10, 12, 14
☐ avoid	☐ 動 避ける	1, 5, 7, 8, 10, 11, 14

B 語彙・表現	品詞 意味	Unit
☐ baggage	☐ 名 荷物	1, 6, 8, 11
☐ be aware of	☐ 〜に気づいている	15
☐ be delighted to	☐ 喜んで〜する	3, 8
☐ be determined to do	☐ do しようと固く決意している	7, 9
☐ be equipped with	☐ 〜が備えられている	8, 11
☐ be expected to do	☐ do すると予想、期待されている	1, 14
☐ be in charge of	☐ 〜の担当である	2
☐ be responsible for	☐ 〜の責任がある	2
☐ be short on	☐ 〜が不足している	3
☐ be stacked	☐ 積み重なっている	8, 10
☐ be supposed to do	☐ do することになっている	2, 13
☐ bear	☐ 動 (称号・名声などを) もつ、掲げる	9
☐ benefit	☐ 名 利益、手当、給付	2, 4, 5, 10, 12, 13, 15
☐ between A and B	☐ A と B の間	5, 6, 7, 8, 12
☐ beverage	☐ 名 飲み物	1
☐ bill	☐ 名 請求書	8
☐ board	☐ 動 搭乗する	12
☐ book	☐ 動 予約する	1, 5, 6, 11, 15
☐ bother	☐ 名 面倒、悩みの種、厄介なこと	8
☐ budget	☐ 名 予算	8, 11, 15
☐ budget proposal	☐ 予算案	2

C 語彙・表現	品詞 意味	Unit
☐ celebrate	☐ 動 祝う	1, 2, 9
☐ celebration	☐ 名 お祝い	2
☐ certification	☐ 名 (資格などの) 認定	10
☐ characteristic	☐ 名 特色、特徴	3
☐ clarify	☐ 動 明確にする	14
☐ climb	☐ 動 登る、昇る	1
☐ clog	☐ 動 詰まらせる、塞ぐ	8
☐ cluttered	☐ 形 雑念とした、散らかった	8
☐ colleague	☐ 名 同僚	1, 5, 7
☐ comfortable	☐ 形 快適な	3, 6, 8, 11
☐ commendable	☐ 形 称賛に値する	11
☐ commercial	☐ 形 商業用の	8, 15
☐ commute	☐ 動 通勤する	8
☐ competitive	☐ 形 競争の、競合する、競争の激しい	10, 15
☐ competitor	☐ 名 競争相手、競合他社	2
☐ complete	☐ 動 完了する	8, 10, 11, 15
☐ complex	☐ 名 複合施設	8

☐ complication	☐ 名 複雑化させる要因、やっかいな問題	7
☐ complimentary	☐ 形 無料の	1, 11
☐ component	☐ 名 部品	15
☐ concern	☐ 名 懸念 （動 心配させる）	7, 8, 10
☐ conclude	☐ 動 結論づける、断定する	2
☐ conduct	☐ 動 行う、実施する	2, 5, 8, 11, 14
☐ confidence	☐ 名 自信	9
☐ confidential	☐ 形 機密の	4
☐ confirm	☐ 動 確認する	3, 6, 7, 9
☐ Congratulations on 物事 .	☐ （物事について）おめでとう。	2
☐ consistent	☐ 形 一貫性のある、矛盾のない	9
☐ construct	☐ 動 建てる、建設する	8
☐ contact	☐ 動 連絡する	1, 8, 9, 10, 11, 13, 15
☐ contemporary	☐ 形 現代の、近代の	13
☐ contract	☐ 名 契約書	7
☐ contribute	☐ 動 貢献する	7, 10, 13
☐ costly	☐ 形 高価な、費用が高い	3
☐ coupon	☐ 名 クーポン	9
☐ coverage	☐ 名 （保証の）補填（範囲）、報道（範囲）	15
☐ crucial	☐ 形 極めて重要な	2, 4, 5, 8, 11, 14
☐ cuisine	☐ 名 料理	3
☐ currently	☐ 副 現在のところ	1, 3, 6, 8, 9, 10, 12

D 語彙・表現　｜品詞｜意味　Unit

☐ deadline	☐ 名 締め切り	2
☐ deal with	☐ 対処する	1, 10, 12
☐ decline	☐ 動 辞退する、低下する	10
☐ dedicated	☐ 形 専門の、専用の、熱心な	7, 11, 13
☐ dedication	☐ 名 献身、専念、熱心さ	2, 7
☐ delay	☐ 動 遅らせる	1, 6, 11, 12
☐ delayed	☐ 形 遅れている	1, 6, 12
☐ demand	☐ 動 要求する	3
☐ demolish	☐ 動 取り壊す	8
☐ departure	☐ 名 出発	11, 12
☐ describe	☐ 動 説明する、記述する、描写する	9, 15
☐ description	☐ 名 説明	15
☐ designate	☐ 動 指定する	11, 12
☐ despite	☐ 前 ～にもかかわらず	5, 11, 12, 14, 15
☐ destination	☐ 名 目的地	1, 6, 11
☐ detail	☐ 名 詳細、細部	2, 7, 14, 15
☐ detector	☐ 名 検知器、探知器、発見器	8
☐ diligently	☐ 熱心に、勤勉に	9
☐ discuss	☐ 動 議論する	2, 7, 12, 14, 15
☐ display	☐ 動 展示している	9, 13
☐ dispose	☐ 動 破棄する	12
☐ distance	☐ 名 距離、間隔	6, 8
☐ donate	☐ 動 寄付する	15
☐ drainpipe	☐ 名 排水管	8
☐ due date	☐ 締切日	4
☐ due to	☐ 前 ～のせいで	1, 2, 3, 5, 6, 8, 12, 15
☐ duration	☐ 名 期間	1
☐ during	☐ 前 ～の間	1, 2, 3, 6, 7, 8, 9, 10, 12, 13, 14

E 語彙・表現　｜品詞｜意味　Unit

☐ earn	☐ 動 稼ぐ、得る	2, 15
☐ eclectic	☐ 形 折衷の、多岐にわたる	3, 6
☐ edit	☐ 動 編集する	4

☐ editor-in-chief	☐ 名 編集長	4	
☐ effort	☐ 名 努力	2, 4, 9, 14	
☐ either A or B	☐ A か B どちらか	3, 8, 11	
☐ electrician	☐ 名 電気技師	8	
☐ electrifying	☐ 形 しびれるような、衝撃的な	13	
☐ eligibility	☐ 名 資格、要件	15	
☐ eliminate	☐ 動 省く、除外する	12	
☐ empty	☐ 動 空にする	15	
☐ enclose	☐ 動 同封する	7	
☐ encourage	☐ 動 促進する、促す	1, 3, 6, 7, 13, 14, 15	
☐ ensure	☐ 動 確実なものにする、保証する	6, 7, 8, 9, 11, 12	
☐ enthusiastic	☐ 形 熱狂的な、熱心な	3, 10	
☐ environmentally friendly	☐ 形 環境にやさしい	14	
☐ equip	☐ 動 備え付ける	8	
☐ equipment	☐ 名 器具、機械	2, 7, 8	
☐ essential	☐ 形 不可欠な	5, 11, 12	
☐ establish	☐ 動 確立する、設立する	12	
☐ evaluation	☐ 名 評価	5, 7	
☐ examine	☐ 動 吟味する、よく調べる	7	
☐ exclusive	☐ 形 排他的な、高級な、独占的な	6, 13	
☐ exhibit	☐ 名 展示物	6	
☐ exhibition	☐ 名 展示	13	
☐ expand	☐ 動 広める、拡張する	4, 14	
☐ expect	☐ 動 期待する	11, 14, 15	
☐ explore	☐ 動 探索する、探検する	1, 6, 13, 14	
☐ exposure	☐ 名 露出、暴露	13	
☐ extend	☐ 動 延ばす、拡大する	1, 11, 13	
☐ extra	☐ 形 追加の	4, 5, 13	

F 語彙・表現	品詞 意味	Unit	
☐ factor	☐ 名 要因、要素	5	
☐ fail to do	☐ do しそこなう	9	
☐ fare	☐ 名 運賃	1	
☐ fasten	☐ 動 装着する、締める	1	
☐ faucet	☐ 名 蛇口	8	
☐ faulty	☐ 形 欠陥のある	8	
☐ feature	☐ 動 目玉とする、特徴とする	8, 13, 15	
☐ feature	☐ 名 目玉となるもの、特徴	8	
☐ feel free to do	☐ 気軽に do する	1, 8, 10	
☐ finalize	☐ 動 終わらせる、まとめる	15	
☐ fix	☐ 動 修理する	1, 8	
☐ flexible	☐ 形 融通のきく	15	
☐ forecast	☐ 名 予報、予測	9, 12	
☐ forward	☐ 動 転送する	5	
☐ foster	☐ 動 育成する	12, 13	
☐ foster	☐ 動 育てる、育成する	12, 13	
☐ free of charge	☐ (手数料などが) 無料で	9	
☐ frequently	☐ 副 頻繁に	15	
☐ furnished	☐ 形 家具付きの	8	
☐ furniture	☐ 名 家具	8	

G 語彙・表現	品詞 意味	Unit	
☐ gain	☐ 動 得る、獲得する	4, 6, 12	
☐ gaming console	☐ 名 ゲーム機器	8, 9	
☐ garbage	☐ 名 ゴミ	12	
☐ gather	☐ 動 集める	2, 14	
☐ generate	☐ 動 生み出す	4	
☐ generously	☐ 副 寛大に	15	

☐ go bankrupt	☐ 破産する		9
☐ gratitude	☐ 名 感謝		14
☐ grocery	☐ 名 食料雑貨品		3, 13
☐ guarantee	☐ 動 保証する		12

H 語彙・表現	品詞 意味	Unit
☐ handle	☐ 動 扱う、操業する	15
☐ hesitate	☐ 動 ためらう、躊躇する	7, 13
☐ highlight	☐ 動 強調する	9
☐ HR (Human Resources)	☐ 人事部	15

I 語彙・表現	品詞 意味	Unit
☐ identification	☐ 名 身分証	1, 7
☐ identify	☐ 動 特定する	1, 7, 15
☐ immediately	☐ 副 すぐに	14, 12
☐ immerse	☐ 動 浸ける、浸す	6
☐ implement	☐ 動 実行する	12
☐ imply	☐ 動 ほのめかす、示唆する	14
☐ improve	☐ 動 改善する、良くなる	5, 6, 7, 11, 14
☐ improvement	☐ 名 改善点、改善	7
☐ in advance	☐ 事前に	1, 3, 6, 11, 13, 14
☐ In case of	☐ ～の場合は	1, 6
☐ in operation	☐ 稼働中、営業中	6
☐ inclement	☐ 形 厳しい、荒れ模様の	6, 12
☐ include	☐ 動 含む	1, 3, 5, 6, 8, 9, 13, 15
☐ inconvenience	☐ 名 不便	6, 8
☐ increase	☐ 名 増加	2, 4, 5, 7, 9
☐ indicate	☐ 動 示す	1, 8, 9, 10
☐ industry	☐ 名 産業、工業、業界	2, 4, 10, 12, 15
☐ infer	☐ 動 推測する	9, 10
☐ initial	☐ 形 当初の、初めの	12
☐ innovative	☐ 形 革新的な	14, 15
☐ inquire	☐ 動 問い合わせる	7, 9, 15
☐ inquiry	☐ 名 問い合わせ	4, 9, 10, 13, 14
☐ insight	☐ 名 洞察力	14
☐ inspect	☐ 動 検査する、点検する	8
☐ inspection	☐ 名 点検、検査	8
☐ inspector	☐ 名 検査員、点検員	8
☐ instead	☐ 副 代わりに、あるいは	5, 7, 13, 15
☐ instruction	☐ 名 説明書、説明	5, 13, 14
☐ intend to *do*	☐ *do* することを意図する	4
☐ intriguing	☐ 形 興味をそそる、興味ある	13
☐ inventory	☐ 名 在庫	7, 9, 15
☐ invest	☐ 動 投資する	4, 8, 12
☐ invoice	☐ 名 請求書	6, 9
☐ issue	☐ 名 問題点	2, 7, 8, 9, 11, 12
☐ itinerary	☐ 名 旅程、行程表	1, 6, 11

J 語彙・表現	品詞 意味	Unit
☐ janitor	☐ 名 清掃員、用務員、管理人	8

K 語彙・表現	品詞 意味	Unit
☐ keep track of	☐ ～の経過を追う、～の記録をつける	9
☐ keynote speaker	☐ 名 基調講演 (演説) 者	2

L 語彙・表現	品詞 意味	Unit
☐ latest	☐ 形 最新の	4, 7, 12, 15
☐ launch	☐ 動 販売開始する、売り出す	4, 9, 12, 15
☐ launch	☐ 名 販売開始、開始	2, 7, 15
☐ lean again	☐ ～にもたれかかる	7
☐ leftovers	☐ 名 残り物	9
☐ legal	☐ 形 法律上の、法的な	15
☐ line up	☐ 並ぶ	13

M 語彙・表現	品詞 意味	Unit
☐ maintain	☐ 動 維持する、維持管理する	2, 5, 11, 13, 15
☐ malfunction	☐ 名 故障	9, 13, 14
☐ manufacturer	☐ 名 製造業者、製造者	9
☐ meaningful	☐ 形 意味のある、有意義な	5, 12
☐ measurements	☐ 名 測定値、測定結果	8
☐ measures	☐ 名 (複数形で) 手段、処置、方法	12
☐ meditation	☐ 名 瞑想	5
☐ mention	☐ 動 言及する	15
☐ minimum	☐ 形 最小の	15
☐ minutes	☐ 名 (複数形で) 議事録	2, 14
☐ modification	☐ 名 修正、変更	15
☐ morale	☐ 名 士気	7, 15
☐ motorized	☐ 形 機械仕掛けの、モーター付きの	8
☐ multiple	☐ 形 複数の	8, 12
☐ multiple	☐ 形 多数の、多様な	8

N 語彙・表現	品詞 意味	Unit
☐ neither A nor B	☐ A も B もどちらも～ない	3, 8
☐ nurture	☐ 動 育てる、育む	13
☐ nutrition	☐ 名 栄養	5

O 語彙・表現	品詞 意味	Unit
☐ offer	☐ 動 提供する	3
☐ on duty	☐ 勤務中	8
☐ on time	☐ 時間通りに	7, 12
☐ open position	☐ 空いている職、欠員	10
☐ operate	☐ 動 操縦する	6, 7
☐ out of stock	☐ 在庫切れ	3, 9, 15
☐ outdated	☐ 形 時代遅れの、古い	8
☐ outstanding	☐ 形 並外れた、極めて優れた	7, 11
☐ overhead compartment	☐ 名 頭上の荷物入れ	1
☐ own	☐ 動 所有する	1, 8

P 語彙・表現	品詞 意味	Unit
☐ participate in	☐ ～に参加する	13, 14
☐ passenger	☐ 名 乗客	6
☐ past	☐ 名 過去	13, 15
☐ pave	☐ 動 舗装する	12
☐ payment	☐ 名 支払い	9
☐ pension	☐ 名 年金	15
☐ performance evaluation	☐ 業績評価、勤務評価	7
☐ personnel	☐ 名 人員、職員、人事	11
☐ pharmaceutical	☐ 形 製薬の	5
☐ pharmaceuticals	☐ 名 製薬、薬品	5
☐ pharmacy	☐ 名 薬局	5
☐ pile up	☐ 積み重ねる	14

☐ place an advertisement	☐ 広告を出す		4, 11
☐ plenty	☐ 名 たくさんのもの		10
☐ plumber	☐ 名 配管工		8
☐ position	☐ 動 置く、配置する		2
☐ potential	☐ 形 潜在的な、将来性のある、見込みのある		2, 8, 12, 14, 15
☐ pour	☐ 動 注ぐ		3
☐ precious	☐ 形 貴重な		5
☐ predict	☐ 動 予測する、予想する		9, 12
☐ preference	☐ 名 好み、嗜好		11
☐ prescribe	☐ 動 処方する		5
☐ prescription	☐ 名 処方箋		5
☐ present	☐ 動 提示する		1, 2, 14
☐ prevent	☐ 動 防ぐ		8, 12, 14
☐ previous	☐ 形 以前の、前の		2, 10
☐ previously	☐ 副 以前に、前に		9
☐ privilege	☐ 名 特権、特典		13
☐ productivity	☐ 名 生産性		7
☐ prohibit	☐ 動 禁止する		1
☐ promote	☐ 動 (物)を販売促進する、(人)を昇進させる		2, 4, 11, 12
☐ promotion	☐ 名 昇進、販売促進活動		2
☐ promotional	☐ 形 販売促進の		2, 4
☐ prompt	☐ 形 迅速な		7, 14
☐ promptly	☐ 副 迅速に		7, 14, 15
☐ property	☐ 名 所有物、財産、資産、不動産		8
☐ proposal	☐ 名 提案		14, 15
☐ prospective	☐ 形 有望な、見込みのある、将来の		15
☐ publish	☐ 動 出版する		4
☐ purchase	☐ 動 購入する		8
☐ purchase	☐ 名 購入		9
☐ put on	☐ 着る (動作動詞)		5

Q 語彙・表現	品詞 意味		Unit
☐ qualification	☐ 名 資格、適正、能力		10
☐ qualified	☐ 形 資質・能力のある、認可を受けている		8, 10
☐ qualify	☐ 動 (人)に資格を与える		10, 15
☐ quality	☐ 名 質、形 上質な		3, 4, 7, 8, 11
☐ quarter	☐ 名 四半期		2, 7, 14

R 語彙・表現	品詞 意味		Unit
☐ range	☐ 名 幅、範囲		2, 8, 15
☐ rapidly	☐ 副 急速に		15
☐ rate	☐ 名 相場、料金		6
☐ reach for	☐ 手を伸ばす		9
☐ real estate	☐ 名 不動産		8
☐ reasonable	☐ 形 お手頃な		3
☐ reception desk	☐ 名 受付		9
☐ recipient	☐ 名 受領者、受益者、受賞者		8
☐ recognition	☐ 名 認識、評価、感謝		2
☐ recognize	☐ 動 認める、評価する		1, 2, 7, 14
☐ recommend	☐ 動 勧める		1, 6, 11
☐ recommendation	☐ 名 お勧め、推奨		3
☐ reconstruct	☐ 動 再工事する、建て替える		8
☐ redeem	☐ 動 引き換える、換金する		7
☐ reduce	☐ 動 減らす		1, 2, 5, 9, 12, 14
☐ reflect	☐ 動 反映する、映す		7
☐ refuse	☐ 動 断る、拒否する		5
☐ regarding	☐ 前 ～について		2
☐ regional	☐ 形 地域の、地方の		12

□ suffer from	□ ～に苦しむ	15
□ suit	□ 動 一致する、似合う	8, 9
□ suitable	□ 形 ふさわしい、適した	5, 11
□ surveillance	□ 名 監視	8
□ survey	□ 名 調査	2, 6, 11, 14
□ sustainability	□ 名 持続可能性	14
□ sweep	□ 動 掃く	4, 12
□ swiftly	□ 副 迅速に	7
□ symptom	□ 名 症状、兆候	5

T 語彙・表現	品詞 意味	Unit
□ take advantage of	□ ～を利用する	15
□ take off	□ 脱ぐ、離陸する	1
□ talent	□ 名 才能	13
□ temporarily	□ 副 一時的に、仮に	8, 11
□ therefore	□ 副 それゆえ	7, 11, 13
□ thoughtful	□ 形 思慮深い、思いやりのある	7
□ throughout	□ 前 ～を通して	8, 13
□ token	□ 名 しるし、記念品、トークン	7, 13
□ toll	□ 名 通行料	1
□ tons of	□ たくさんの	15
□ translate	□ 動 翻訳する	4
□ transport	□ 動 運ぶ、輸送する	6, 11
□ trust	□ 名 信頼	9, 13
□ tuition	□ 名 授業料、月謝	15

U 語彙・表現	品詞 意味	Unit
□ under construction	□ 工事中	8, 12
□ undergo	□ 動 受ける、経験する	7, 11
□ unique	□ 形 独自の	11, 13
□ unpack	□ 動 荷をほどく、荷物を出す	8
□ unstable	□ 形 不安定な、落ち着かない	7
□ up to	□ 前 最高～まで	6
□ upcoming	□ 形 今後の、今からある	2, 4, 7, 13
□ utilize	□ 動 活用する、役立たせる	13, 15

V 語彙・表現	品詞 意味	Unit
□ valuable	□ 形 貴重な、価値ある	1, 11, 14
□ various	□ 形 様々な	4, 6, 10, 12, 15
□ vase	□ 名 花瓶、つぼ	8
□ vehicle	□ 名 車両	6, 8
□ vending machine	□ 自動販売機	5
□ venue	□ 名 会場	10, 12, 13

W 語彙・表現	品詞 意味	Unit
□ wander	□ 動 歩き回る、ぶらつく	6
□ warehouse	□ 名 倉庫	9
□ warn	□ 動 警告する、予告する、前もって知らせる	7
□ warranty	□ 名 保証	9
□ wear	□ 動 身につけている、着用している	1, 4, 5, 9, 10
□ wearable	□ 形 身に着けられる、着用できる	7
□ whether A or B	□ 接 A か B か	3, 6, 11, 13, 15
□ wholesaler	□ 名 卸売業者	9
□ windowpane	□ 名 窓ガラス	8
□ within	□ 前 ～以内	1, 5, 6, 8, 11, 12, 13
□ worth	□ 形 価値がある	6, 8, 15

Maximize Your Score on the TOEIC® L&R Test
シーン別で学ぶ TOEIC® L&R テスト総合対策

2024 年 4 月 10 日　初版第 1 刷発行

著　者　　鶴岡公幸／佐藤千春／Matthew Wilson

発 行 者　森　信久
発 行 所　株式会社　松 柏 社
　　　　　〒102 − 0072　東京都千代田区飯田橋 1 − 6 − 1
　　　　　TEL 03 (3230) 4813（代表）
　　　　　FAX 03 (3230) 4857
　　　　　http://www.shohakusha.com
　　　　　e-mail: info@shohakusha.com

本文レイアウト・組版　株式会社インターブックス
装　幀　　小島トシノブ（NONdesign）
印刷・製本　中央精版印刷株式会社
ISBN978-4-88198-792-6
略　号＝ 792
Copyright © 2024 Tomoyuki Tsuruoka, Chiharu Sato and Matthew Wilson